Ian Maclaren

The Cure of Souls

Lyman Beecher lectures on preaching at Yale University, 1896

Ian Maclaren

The Cure of Souls
Lyman Beecher lectures on preaching at Yale University, 1896

ISBN/EAN: 9783337144425

Printed in Europe, USA, Canada, Australia, Japan

Cover: Foto ©Thomas Meinert / pixelio.de

More available books at **www.hansebooks.com**

LYMAN BEECHER LECTURES ON PREACHING
AT YALE UNIVERSITY

1896

BY

JOHN WATSON, M.A., D.D.

NEW YORK
DODD, MEAD & COMPANY
1896

TO THE

REV. GEORGE P. FISHER, D.D., LL.D.,

Professor of Ecclesiastical History and
Dean of the Faculty of Theology
in Yale University

IN RESPECT

FOR HIS DISTINGUISHED ATTAINMENTS

IN GRATITUDE

FOR HIS THOUGHTFUL KINDNESS

PREFACE.

IT was the excellent custom of a Theological College which from time to time has sent forth learned and brilliant scholars as well as many ordinary men, to invite ministers of age and reputation to inform the students on the practical work of their calling. Their addresses used to fill the College with admiration, because of the eloquence and distinction of the speakers, but one student they reduced to despair. He had secretly hoped for some account of the difficulties and dangers which were likely to beset the path of one who, like himself, represented the average man.

What he desired was never given, and he was in due course ordained and entered on the work of the holy ministry. As he paid his bitter premiums to experience, it came to him that some day he would write a little book in which he might be able to save some brother minister from humiliation and suffering, and this he has now tried to do according to the measure of his ability.

It is not likely, however, that the writer would have had the courage of his intention had not the Faculty of Theology in Yale University done him the unmerited honour of an invitation to deliver the Lyman Beecher lectures on Preaching, and had accepted from him simpler service than that which was fittingly rendered by his distinguished predecessors in the lectureship.

CONTENTS

CHAPTER I

THE GENESIS OF A SERMON . . . . PAGE 3

CHAPTER II

THE TECHNIQUE OF A SERMON 37

CHAPTER III

PROBLEMS OF PREACHING 65

CHAPTER IV

THEOLOGY THE THEORY OF RELIGION . . 101

CHAPTER V

THE NEW DOGMA 131

CHAPTER VI

THE MACHINERY OF A CONGREGATION . . 161

CHAPTER VII

THE WORK OF A PASTOR 207

CHAPTER VIII

THE PUBLIC WORSHIP OF GOD 245

CHAPTER IX

THE MINISTER'S CARE OF HIMSELF . . . 275

THE GENESIS OF A SERMON

CHAPTER I

THE GENESIS OF A SERMON

It lies upon the minister of Christ to care for the souls of his people from house to house; to spare no pains that divine service be beautiful and reverent; to afford to the young every useful means of religious culture; to move his congregation unto such good works as lie to their hand: but it is well for him to remember that the most critical and influential event in the religious week is the sermon. History bears unanimous testimony on this point. When the Evangel ceased, or fell into contempt, the Church grew weak and corrupt. When the Evangel asserted its ancitent authority, the Church arose and put on her 'beautiful garments.' No power in human experience has wrought such mighty works as the spoken word : it has beaten down impiety, taught righteousness, given freedom to the oppressed, and created nations. Before Knox, armed with this sword of God, hosts fled, and he reigned in the pulpit of St. Giles as a king upon his throne : and if you go into the roots of things, was not the American nation founded on brave, wholesome speech? It is the prophet who has roused the race from ignoble sleep, has fired its imagination with lofty ideals, has nerved it for costly sacrifices, has led it to victory. It is the prophet, above all, who, under Christ, has laid the foundations of the Church in every land, has restored her after periods of decay, has filled her with courage and hope. He is the teacher, comforter, fosterer, defender of his brethren, and therefore the chief office to which any man can be called is to declare the Will of God, and especially the Evangel of Christ.

THE GENESIS OF A SERMON

No one can exaggerate the opportunity given to a preacher when, on the morning of the first day of the week, he ascends the pulpit and faces a congregation who are gathered in the name of Jesus, and wait to hear what he has to say to them concerning the things which are unseen and eternal. Each man carries his own burden of unbelief, sorrow, temptation, care, into the House of God, and the preacher has to hearten all; for, indeed, the work of the pulpit in our day is not so much to teach or define as to stimulate and encourage. That minister who receives a body of people more or less cast down, and wearied in the great battle of the soul, and sends them forth full of good cheer and enthusiasm, has done his work and deserved well of his people. He has shown himself a true shepherd, and he had not done this service without knowing both the Will of God and the life of man, without draining a wide watershed of experience—from high hills where the soul has been alone with God, and from deep valleys where the soul has tasted the agonies of life—into the stream that shall be the motive power of many lives on the plains beneath.

If the sermon be in its degree a prophetical utterance, then it must be in its essence a mystery. What the prophet tells forth he must first be told, but how God uncovers His servant's ear and whispers His message no one can explain. The true preacher is distinguished by a certain demonic influence—a divine passion—which breathes through the thought, the words, the very manner, which cannot be described, which is felt in the marrow of the bones. This is the only infallible sign of a prophet; it is the baptism of the Holy Ghost, and about such secret and sacred things it becometh one to be silent and to fear. When one passes from vision to utterance, then it is possible and

THE GENESIS OF A SERMON

useful to inquire in what way a sermon comes into existence and grows into perfection. People will see the finished product, but as a rule they are rigidly excluded from the manufactory, which no one is allowed to enter except on business. Perhaps it might be better for a minister to take hearers into his confidence about the production of sermons, both because they would be very much interested, and because they would have a more intelligent sympathy with the preacher. They would be delivered from various blinding and irritating errors, such as confounding an unread with an extempore sermon, while they ought to know that the former may have cost a week's study, and have been written word for word, and that the latter, having cost nothing, neither time nor thought, is worth nothing, and for purposes of description ought to be described as 'ex-trumpery.' Certainly it must be useful for practical men, whose life-work is to be preaching, to compare notes on the various methods of preparation, believing that as the blessing of the Divine Spirit will only rest on the outcome of hard, honest work, the more thorough and skilful that work is, the more likely is it to be crowned with prosperity.

A sermon, I submit, is the result of six processes, and the first is *Selection*.

Curious stories are afloat regarding this process, which suggest that in some quarters it must be very imperfectly understood. It is said that the preacher will sometimes spend the week seeking for a text, and be only delivered from despair on Saturday night by lighting on a verse, in some minor prophet, which has a catching sound, and looks as if it would lend itself to a 'memorable' division. People remark next day that it was wonderful how much he brought out of it, but they might have more shrewdly considered how much he put into it. This is speaking by sleight of hand, and the preacher is simply a verbal juggler performing in a sacred place. Others deprecate the very idea of selecting a subject, and declare that if ministers only had faith it would be given unto them—one allowing his Bible to open at a certain place, and so obtaining his text by lot; another waiting till Sunday morning, and even till he is in the pulpit, for guidance. An expert in sermons can recognise this type at once, partly by the preacher using a pocket Bible, from which he can eke out the time by copious references, and partly by an introduction enough to alarm even courageous hearers, explaining how the preacher had been led by a special providence to his theme, but chiefly by the style, which is a series of tacks through a dead sea of pious platitudes in hope of catching a breeze that will bring the ship to some haven. This method is commended in theory as showing a proper dependence on the Holy Ghost, and in public is usually discredited by the thinness of the sermon and the smallness of the congregation. In Scotland this preacher is identified with delicate and suggestive sarcasm, as a 'gude cratur,' and he is really the ghost of mysticism, the caricature of Evangelism.

A certain practical and robust mind has no difficulty in finding texts, because, within very wide limits, it can manipulate any text in a reputable and solid fashion. As it is the duty of this artisan to furnish two sermons for next Sunday, he goes out, say on Tuesday, into the Bible as into a woodyard, and selects, with due deliberation, suitable material, and then, bit by bit, he constructs the discourses, measuring, sawing, planing, and joining in a very deft manner, and finishing with a polish composed of one part spirit, crude and fiery, and three parts thick sweet oil. This workman has lying by him a set of simple designs which suffice for anything he is likely to attempt, and, to do him justice, he is not given to fancies. If his subject be a doctrine, say Faith, then he uses No. I.: (*a*) The origin of Faith; (*b*) The nature of Faith; (*c*) The object of Faith; (*d*) The effects of Faith. And so for Hope or Love. But if his subject be a Scripture hero, say Moses, then he takes down Design II.: (*a*) Moses' parentage; (*b*) His training; (*c*) His work; (*d*) His death (this optional, according to circumstances); (*e*) His character, with lessons. No charge of slackness can be brought against this preacher, for he always turns out a piece of tradesmanlike work; but it still remains, if one dare say it in the face of men of reputation and position in the Church, that there is surely some difference in principle between the construction of a table and a sermon. He that can preach about anything can really preach about nothing. A sermon is more than a cunning creation; it is an inspiration, not so much dead stuff laboriously fitted together, but a tree whose leaf is green, which yieldeth its fruit in due season.

It is not the man who selects the text—that is not the inwardness of the fact—it is the text which selects the man. As the minister was busy with study, or as he sat by the bedside of the sick, or as he walked the crowded street, or as he wandered over the purple heather, or—such things have happened, the grace of God being sovereign — as he endured in a Church Court, the truth, clad in a text, which is the more or less perfect dress of the Spirit, suddenly appeared and claimed his acquaintance. It seemed to him that they had met in the past, as one is haunted by the idea that he has known some one before he has ever seen him; and he will be right, for there is a pre-established harmony between that particular truth and his soul. He is the man to declare it to the world, and it is the truth to arouse his powers. The minister ought at once to put down this idea in a large book, with six pages at its command, for they will be needed. Some slight note may be made of this first meeting and its incidents, and then a friendship—shall I say courtship?—begins, which may last for years before the world knows anything about the matter. Sometimes the idea immediately fascinates, but it does not follow that its marriage-day should be hastened; it is desirable that acquaintance should first grow into knowledge. Sometimes the idea actually repels, and the minister vows he will have nothing to do with it; but he must not be too sure, for hate is a form of love. One by one those ideas that have come out from a multitude and seized the mind will grow into sermons, and meanwhile any glimpses of them in quiet hours and any chance interview with them must be recorded. Such notes are all prolegomena to the discourse, pencil sketches from which the picture will be painted. 'How long does it take to prepare a sermon?' is an ambiguous question. If you mean to write the manuscript, then a day may suffice; if you mean to think a sermon, then it may be ten years. What time goes to the making of wine? In a few months the vine springs and flourishes and bears her grapes, and in a few days they are trodden into the new wine. But a glass of Madeira—it has made voyages, and been tossed up and down in the hold of vessels, and lain in dark cool cellars for half a century, and so it has come to mellow perfection. New thought is almost sure to be crude and yeasty, and therefore wise and charitable deliverances can hardly be expected of young preachers, because their thought has not yet had time to ripen. It is enough if it be strong and rich; fineness and fragrance will come with age.

As the years go on, a preacher's success will largely depend on his accumulated resources of sermon material—not the gold which has been minted and now is in circulation, nor even what is going through the mill, but the ore in sight within the mine. When he discovers that the reserve is being exhausted, then it would be wise to close production before he has to fall back on low-grade ore, and to strike a deeper level, where new and richer veins will often be revealed. The worst condition for sermon-making is where the minister lives from hand to mouth, and the best where he longs to live to the age of the patriarchs, because he is certain that he will never be able in a short modern lifetime to deliver one-tenth of the living thoughts in his brain.

The second process is *Separation*.

THE CURE OF SOULS

When the minister turns over the leaves of the book with his reserves, and settles in his mind that a certain theme is ready for preaching, he has before him a hard week's work, and if he stints his care at any point then he will simply fling away his treasure. It happens sometimes that a sermon fails because although the carving is excellent the wood is worthless, but just as often because although the wood be richly grained the artist has scamped his labour. A noble and inspiring idea is only a promise of success, and the issue hangs on skill and patience. The idea does not come alone, but is accompanied by ninety-nine others with which it is connected by blood, and to which it is naturally attached. One cannot undertake a more delicate task than to wean an idea from its relatives, but this is absolutely necessary in the interests of the sermon. It is one thing for the preacher to woo and win a single idea, and to set up house with it in undisturbed company, and another to have all his wife's relations landed on him. Some sermons are crowded with related doctrines—the connection is often very slender—which brawl together and jostle one another in a very confusing and irritating fashion. If a preacher thinks it wise, he may in an hour compass the circle of Christian doctrine; but it goes without saying that no subject will be more than touched, and that every sermon will be a repetition of the last. Surely half an hour can be fully used in showing, say, the absolute and unfettered grace of divine forgiveness, without travelling into the doctrines either of sin or the atonement,—which in such a case ought to be implicit,—and a preacher may very well enforce the duty of trust in God, without going into all the problems that arise under the head of faith.

'He's a good preacher'—a Highland gamekeeper was describing his minister,—

'but he scatters terribly.' It is the difference between a single rifle bullet which, if it hits, kills, and a charge of small shot which only peppers. Take one sin that happens to be mine and other men's, and let the preacher confine himself, say, to pride, and it will be strange if he does not arrest and shame me, but let him throw in a dozen other sins and I shall be unmoved. My medicine is held in too large a solution. A sermon ought to be a monograph and not an encyclopædia, an agency for pushing one article, not a general store where one can purchase anything from a button to a coffin. There are minds so comprehensive and agile that they can play with half a dozen ideas in one sermon and delight an audience—making one idea illuminate another, and using the combined force of opposite ideas to produce the desired effect; but for the average man with whom we are concerned the handling of one is a sufficient strain.

THE GENESIS OF A SERMON

[There are three degrees—the preacher below par, who can speak for an hour without a single idea; the preacher above par, who will charm us for an hour with a coruscation of ideas; and the preacher just at par, who does his duty in something less than forty minutes by one distinct idea.]

Two reasons may be suggested for casual sermons—where the speaker saunters from door to door—and the first is simply slackness and laziness. He has not set himself in a strenuous and persevering fashion to identify and isolate his idea. This is a forenoon's work, and four hours has not been wasted if by one o'clock the student can rise from his desk, saying, What I have been thinking about for years, and am going to preach about on Sunday, is not that, nor that, but just this—one crisp, clean-cut, complete idea.

[Compensation for this long travail, with its apparently limited result, can be found in the waste products which are thrown off—all of which can be utilised at some future date. The débris in cutting out your angel from the marble may afford material for many a little Psyche.]

Another reason may be the supposed necessity for safeguarding one's creed by insisting on opposite truths in one sermon. It were dangerous, it is supposed, to insist upon Christ's humanity without a long passage on His Divinity, or to enforce works without exalting faith in the same breath. Surely the time has come for putting this policy of fear into the pillory and delivering young men from its tyranny. It is insulting to the preacher to suppose that because he journeyed towards the south pole to-day he denies the north pole, and exasperating to the hearers to be hurried backwards and forwards in opposite directions lest they should rush to extremes. Preacher and hearers should give themselves to one idea with as much

THE GENESIS OF A SERMON

concentration as if there were not another in the universe of thought. This is to focus the mind.

The third process is *Illumination*.

And now the student sets his bare, cold, lifeless idea in the light of all he has read, has seen, has felt, has suffered. He has mercilessly withdrawn it from its environment that it may be his own ; now he restores it to the wide world that it may live, and according to the wideness and richness of the student's world will be the glow, the red blood of his sermon. He goes on a marriage tour with his bride. It is now that he garners the benefit of his intellectual, spiritual, and human culture, and has an unspeakable advantage over the ablest Philistine. Those mornings given to Plato, that visit to Florence where he got an insight into Italian art, that hard-won trip to Egypt the birthplace of civilisation, his sustained acquaintance with Virgil, his by-study of physical science, his taste in music, the subtlest and most religious of the arts, all now rally to his aid. Greek philosophy clarifies the thinking, Andrea Del Sarto illustrates it; a poet suggests a musical line; Faraday points out a parallel between the worlds of nature and spirit. He is unfortunate whose thoughts are untouched by poetry and unfortified by ancient wisdom, over whose study the sky is ever grey and dull. An idea may be his, but his impression of it will be cold and colourless. On the other hand, he must have some reserve and self-denial on whose mind the sun beats strongly. It is possible to confuse and blot out an idea by excess of light, so that amid pictures, rivers, pyramids, sunsets, science, poetry, history, and drama, the hearer does not catch the one message that the preacher had for his soul. One blind after another has to be pulled down on certain brilliant and opulent minds before an idea, however grand and august, has its right place.

[Travel must be used very skilfully and sparingly, because the Righi and the Bay of Naples are not now unknown to a congregation. On the whole, it may be also better for the average man not to go to the Holy Land for the sake of his people unless he has great self-control. His personal experiences will make even the Mount of Olives a terror, and his interpolated explanation from 'what I saw' will desecrate the noblest passages in the Gospels. Some congregations who sent their ministers to the Holy Land in the kindness of their hearts, would now pay twice the cost cheerfully to obliterate the journey from the memory of the good man, and to rescue, say the fifteenth of St. Luke, from illustrative anecdotes.]

The fourth process is *Meditation*.

And now for two days this idea must

be removed from the light, where reason and imagination have their sphere, and be hidden away in the dark chambers of the soul. This is not an intellectual proposition to be asserted and proved, or a fancy to be tracked out and exhibited. This is a spiritual truth to be commended to faith, a living principle to be enforced on conscience. It must, therefore, be first imprinted on the preacher's soul till it has become a part of his own being, before he can really understand or declare it. One reason why many masterly sermons fail is that they have never had the benefit of this process; therefore they are clear, interesting, eloquent, but helpless. They do not make way, and lay hold of hearers, because they have never conquered the speaker. He has not been horrified at this sin, has not felt this trial, has not seen this Christ during the week through the sympathy of the soul. The preacher, to succeed, must be Peter as he denies his

THE GENESIS OF A SERMON

Lord, and Mary as her brother dies, and the Syrian woman as she sees Christ yields to her irresistible importunity. This baptism into the heart of a subject, till the preacher and sermon be of one blood, is a secret process that can go on as the minister does his work, but is much accelerated on his quiet walks and in his lonely hours. Unfortunately for us, at the close of the nineteenth century, with its competition, sensationalism, externalism, and endless bustle, meditation is a lost art, like the making of Venetian glass and certain painters' pigments. It is not reading, nor thinking, nor praying; it is brooding, a spiritual experience, where the subject is hidden in the soul as leaven in three measures of meal till all be leavened. What we have chiefly to learn for the work of the holy ministry, in our day, is not how to criticise, nor how to read, nor how to speak, nor how to organise, but how to meditate, in order that present-day sermons may add to their brightness and interest the greater qualities of the past, depth of experience, and an atmosphere of peace.

It will be observed that not one sentence of the sermon has as yet been composed, and so on Friday morning the minister proceeds to the fifth process—*Elaboration.*

He now sits down at his desk and places before him thirty small pieces of paper. [This is an *obiter dictum*, for if one should say, 'Why not two sheets of foolscap?' I can only express amazement at his commonplace contrivance. My plan, as will appear, is much more ingenious, and is an invention. It is with us, as with the medical profession, a rule to patent nothing, but to offer every discovery for the use of our brethren.]

Let each thought, illustration, application, that has occurred to the minister under his idea be committed to one of

THE GENESIS OF A SERMON

those scraps. Just as one remembers them; in no sequence—a mere mob of recollections. It is, of course, taken for granted that each must be, as it were, the legitimate child of that idea. No vagrants are to be picked up and adopted.

[For these the minister has another book, a sort of Foundling Asylum for homeless and nameless thoughts, but out of which some very good children may come.]

When the heap is complete, behold the raw material, selected, picked, dyed, ready now for the mill that shall weave the loose disconnected threads into pattern and cloth, or, if it please you, to revert to a former image, the print must now be taken off the negative. This heap of thought-stuff is as an alphabet, with every letter there, but all unarranged. It is the student's business to spread the letters out on his table, and to survey them carefully till he lights on A and B and C, on to

X Y Z. For he knows that thought follows a certain order, and it is the same order in the mind of a peasant as a philosopher, only in the former case some of the letters are wanting—blank spaces—and some are dim. Educated people resent a sermon where A comes in the middle of the alphabet and S precedes M, and they are not appeased by the fact that they have had all the letters somehow; and it may be worth saying that people without culture are almost as dissatisfied by a disorderly sermon. Hearers have an action of damages against a preacher who rambles and comes again on his own track, because it is disheartening to follow a guide whose progress is a zigzag, and because it is plain that he has scamped his work.

[Certain fertile and original minds are what gardeners call 'sports,' that is, they do not come under ordinary laws. They are incapable of reasoned or connected thinking, and their productions ought to be printed in paragraphs with asterisks between—each an aphorism, an observation, an illustration—flashes of brilliant light for which we are thankful.]

Our average man must not claim the privilege of vagrant genius; he must wrestle and sweat, placing, reviewing, transposing till the way stands fair and open from Alpha to Omega — a clean, straight furrow from end to end of the field, a chain of single links which when put to the test holds. Something there will be before A, especially when a man is young—an introduction which used to extend back to the creation of the world and the purposes of God, and now embraces the latest results of criticism on the book from which the text is taken. Whether our fathers liked to approach, say the Son of God, through an underground passage of theological archæology may be doubtful, but it is certain their children have no wish to arrive at an ethical principle of prophecy through a museum of the higher criticism. This generation desires to be ushered into the subject of the day without wearisome preliminaries, and nothing will more certainly take the edge off the appetite than a laborious preface. Very likely it must be written, or else the minister could not get further, but it ought then to be burned as having served its purpose. It is really getting up steam, and there is no use in inviting passengers on board till the vessel is ready to start.

Something there will be after Z — a striking and eloquent peroration, and, although this sounds cruel to a degree, this ought also to be suppressed. When the sermon has culminated after a natural fashion, it ought to end, leaving its effect to rest not on rhetoric but on truth. There may be times when for effect the sermon may cease suddenly some letters before Z, because the audience has surrendered without terms and the sermon has served its purpose.

When a speaker is pleading a great cause, and sees hard-headed men glaring before them with such ferocity that every one knows they are afraid of breaking down, let him stop in the middle of a paragraph and take the collection, and if he be declaring the Evangel, and a certain tenderness comes over the faces of the people, let him close his words to them and call them to prayer. Speech can be too lengthy, too formal, too eloquent, too grammatical. For one to lose his toilsome introduction, in which he happened to mention two Germans, with quotations, and his twice-written conclusion, in which he had that pretty fancy from Tennyson, is hard to flesh and blood. It is worse than the 'Massacre of the Innocents'—it is infanticide; but in those sacrifices of self the preacher's strength lies, on them the blessing of God rests. Broken sentences, when the speaker could not continue, unfinished sermons, when the Spirit of God was working powerfully, have wrought marvels beyond all the wisdom of the schools.

If Saturday be given to the actual writing of the sermon (which comes under technique) then there remains one other process, which is reserved for Sunday morning, and that is *Revision*.

No photograph quite represents the face that was taken, or leaves the studio untouched. Certain lines have to be modified, certain blots to be removed. It will be a very gracious sermon that needs no retouching. Line by line the sermon has to be read over with the faces of his congregation before him, so that the minister may hear how it sounds in the living environment. Many things are incisive and telling, clever and sparkling on paper, which we feel will not do face to face. They are now too telling, too clever. A well-turned epigram, which cost much oil : but that white-haired saint will misunderstand it. Our St. John must not be grieved. So it must go. A very impressive word of the new scientific coinage : what can yon sempstress make of it? Rich people have many pleasures, she has only her church. Well, she shall have it without rebate : the big word is erased—half a line in mourning. A shrewd hit at a certain weakness : but that dear old mother, whose house is a refuge for orphans and all kinds of miserables, it is just possible she may be hurt. The minister had not thought of her till he said the words with Dorcas sitting in her corner. Another black line in the fair manuscript. This exposure of narrowness is at any rate justified : but the minister sees one face redden, and its owner is as true a man as God ever made. It is left out too. Somewhat strong that statement : an adjective shall be omitted : some people have a delicate sense of words. This quip may excite a laugh : better not—it may hinder the force of the next passage on Jesus. The sermon seems to be losing at every turn in harmony, vivacity, richness, ease ; it is gaining in persuasiveness, understanding, sympathy, love : it is losing what is human and gaining what is divine ; and after that sermon is delivered, and has passed into men's lives, the preacher will bless God for every word he removed.

He stands before his people now in the supreme moment of his life, and a sense of the solemnity of his duty overcomes him, so that they see him hesitate between the text and the sermon. Let them pray with one accord that upon this frail brother man, on whom God has laid such a work, the Holy Ghost may descend, and the same Spirit make tender their hearts within them.

THE TECHNIQUE OF A SERMON

CHAPTER II

THE TECHNIQUE OF A SERMON

WHEN a student of a certain college dear unto my heart preached in a city church in the former time, his friends went to hear him and offered him the benefit of an impartial criticism next morning at the common-room fire. Faults were pointed out with frank and incisive speech, but only one was considered unpardonable. If the sermon had been uninteresting, and the congregation had slumbered, there was a strong presumption that the preacher had been thoughtful, and if he rectified some ancient notions with many technical and unintelligible words, then it was certain that he had been profound, —one who in course of time and patient continuance in profundity might climb into a Professor's chair. [It is said unto this day, concerning a preacher whom congregations will not abide, 'He ought to be made a Professor'; but of late the Church has rather inclined to the policy of putting brilliant preachers into theological chairs — with doubtful results, because the pulpit loses in strength, while the new Professor is apt to be described in scholarly circles as showy.] But if the misguided student gripped the people by dealing with things in their experience, and using the language of the market-place, then he was stigmatised as 'popular,' and in the case of his having stirred the people unto one of the deep human emotions, every right-minded man knew that he was a charlatan of the first water.

Within a stone's-throw of this place of learning was a Court of Justice where educated men were daily practising the same art of public speech, but where an-

THE TECHNIQUE OF A SERMON

other canon of success obtained. If any barrister, being intrusted with a case, had plunged into a historical or critical dissertation on a particular law, it would have been his last brief, and the curious thing is that his fellow-barristers would have given him scant praise. His business, as he took it, was to strip his case of all legal technicalities, and to lay it before the jury in such persuasive language as to win their suffrages. His aim was not to receive the approval of scientific experts, but to gain a verdict. If he descended to claptrap, or said what was not true, then he suffered loss, but within the conditions of fair reasoning he used any means that seemed likely to win the jury, and in proportion as he could honestly bring twelve fellow-citizens to his view he was counted successful.

The preacher also addresses a jury of say five hundred people, and whether his subject be sin or righteousness, doctrine or duty, he has to bring them to his way of thinking, and persuade them to believe his message. If he talks above their heads, or delivers himself of dead information, or airs his own conceits, or raises vain questions, or bores them with obsolete doctrines, then he misses his chance, and in spite of his learning or acuteness or piety he is a failure. 'I once heard him preach,' said a man of letters, who was referring to a distinguished clergyman, 'and it was an excellent sermon—about the best in my experience.' 'His text?' 'I have not the ghost of an idea, nor do I remember his argument, nor anything he said.' 'How do I know that it was good?' 'Because before we left church he convinced us that God was love. I am not sure that I believe that to-day, but I believed it that morning.—Yes,' he added, 'that man deserves his name, for he knows his business.'

Regarding the substance of his message,

the preacher must be a prophet, declaring what he believes with all his heart; regarding its form, he must be a barrister, delivering what he has to say in a skilful and cunning manner.

Now, the art of public speech has six canons, and the first is—

Unity. If the sermon is to consist of one idea, then the style must play with this idea for thirty minutes, so that the people never escape from its sphere of influence, are never wearied by it, but that with every minute the idea grows more intelligible, reasonable, winsome. Whether in such circumstances a sermon ought to be parcelled out into heads is an important question. Three detached sermonettes do not make one sermon; but, on the other hand, a handful of observations tied together by a text are not an organic whole. It all depends on whether the heads advance, ascend, cumulate, or are independent, disconnected, parallel. Heads are either water-tight compartments, in which case you cannot pass from one to the other, and are exasperated by the iron door, or they are floors of a tower, in which case one will not halt till he reaches the top, because with every fresh ascent he gets a wider view. It was once the fashion to have heads, and now it is the fashion not to have heads; but much can be said for the former way. One likes rests and points of departure.

If any one desires to lodge an idea in the minds of his hearers he must learn the secret of artistic repetition, by which the same thing is said over and over again, but cast into a new dress on each reappearance. Sometimes it is an intellectual proposition, and the matter is argued to the great delight of the hard-headed people, who begin to think there is something in this idea. Sometimes it is an illustration which appears to simple folk, and they fall in love with the idea.

Sometimes it is an application, and practical people are taken by storm. Now this Pretean shape arrests the conscience, now it convinces the reason, now it captivates the imagination, and now it reinforces the will. People to whom it was a stranger become accustomed to its face and receive it in the end as a friend. It is by this ingenious and elaborate reiteration that popular speakers influence the average man and move him at their will. The citadel has to be carried at the point of the bayonet, and yields only at the sixth assault. The speaker, we shall suppose, feels bound to enforce the ever fresh and needful commonplace, 'That what we sow we shall reap.' [It is a sign of weakness to shrink from the commonplace and to take refuge in a fantastic originality. Any one can have an entirely new and very striking view of familiar scenery by standing on his head.] The statement is made to the audience clearly and decidedly, that reaping will follow sowing, and a hearer awakes to the fact that some one is speaking; which is something gained, for it will prevent him conducting his business in church. But the ambition of the preacher is not exhausted. He now insists that no one can break the connection between sowing and reaping, and the hearer has identified him as a man with some kind of message. So far good: the two are now face to face. Wheat produces wheat, tares produce tares. It is evident the preacher has got hold of some truth about consequences in life, and the hearer is resolved that he will have it out of him. It would be wisdom for every man to examine his sowing, since the reaping is beyond his changing. The hearer is inclined to believe that the preacher is asserting the possibility of changing tares into wheat, and he is prepared to deny the statement.

THE TECHNIQUE OF A SERMON

Full of hope, the preacher makes a sally into life to support his principle: the hearer sees at last what he is after, and takes the new position into judgment. Now the preacher throws off his coat for a final effort, and accomplishes his end. The hearer is finally convinced that the harvest in autumn hangs on the seed-time in spring, and mentions the discovery freely next day as one he made some years ago. The preacher may then congratulate himself, for no teacher is satisfied till he has so lodged an idea in the mind that his people claim it as his own. He has an ample reward for his pains, when his people some day turn upon him and threaten to rend him for criticising an idea which he himself taught them in the agony of his soul, and which they guard jealously as their personal property.

The second canon is *Lucidity*, which lays people under a debt of gratitude. When a willing and intelligent hearer can follow a speaker from his first sentence to his last without effort, he is almost prepared to agree with everything he says, even although he should assert that the earth is square. If a distinguished preacher be conspicuously lucid we may be for a moment disappointed, judging the transparent water, where the delicate seaweed is seen on the rock below, to be shallow; but in the next we are charmed, because water so deep has been so clear and revealing, like unto St. John's Gospel. Lucidity is never to be confounded with simplicity: the former is a quality of style, the latter of thought, and it sometimes happens that what is childish in idea may be unintelligible in expression, while what is profound in idea may be plain to a child. Too much can be made of simplicity, and one is moved to protest against that patronising phrase, 'the simple Gospel.' The Gospel is everlasting: it is mighty; it is divine: it is glorious;—it is not simple.

It could not be, for the Gospel declares the nature of God, the sin of man, the way of life, and the wonders of the unseen world. Nor must the Gospel be degraded by childish arguments, ignoble illustrations, and base appeals. But the Gospel is lucid in the mouth of the apostles, most of all from the lips of Jesus, and it is fair to demand that it be always preached as in the fifteenth of St. Luke or the last chapters of St. John.

Lucid speaking is dependent on clear thinking, and no one can expect to put any subject clearly before his fellows till he has seen it himself from beginning to end. It is a pleasant occupation to watch the clouds wreathing themselves around a mountain, and one catches lovely glimpses when the sun shines through the mist. But billowy masses of words, with an occasional exquisite revelation, is not profitable preaching, and, at its best, it can never hold the people who are not especially poetical, but have a passionate desire to know what the speaker means. Poetry is not by any means a good discipline for clarifying the mind, but it would be a good rule that every minister should have a thorough training in mental philosophy, and continue his reading in that development until he has reached middle age. He must be very careful, however, to keep philosophy out of his sermons, where it is an alien and an offence.

[A course of sermons on the metaphysics of faith, followed by another on the philosophy of prayer, will go far to make infidels of a congregation. One wants his drinking-water taken through a filter-bed, but greatly objects to gravel in his glass.]

The third canon is *Beauty;* and there is no audience which does not expect a certain elevation of style in religious speech, and which does not resent what is vulgar or technical. A preacher does not conciliate an uneducated audience by the use of slang or lapses into buffoonery, nor does he please cultured people by scholastic terms. People have an instinct about what they like to hear from the pulpit, and their desire is the language of the home and the market-place, raised to its highest power and glorified. Every strong and clean word used of the people as they buy and sell, joy and sorrow, labour and suffer, should be in the preacher's store, but he should add thereto splendid and gracious words from Milton and Spenser, from Goldsmith and Addison, and other masters of the English tongue. The ground may be a homely and serviceable grey, but through it should run a thread of gold. People have a just satisfaction in seeing their best words serving in great affairs, and receive a shock of delight when now and again a word of royal carriage mingles with the throng.

Certain preachers enrich their sermons

with quotations, and a stately line has often fitly crowned an argument. But this habit calls for delicacy and reticence. When the sentence of some loved writer occurs to one as he is thinking out his discourse, and he uses it as the expression of his own mind, then it becomes a part of the pattern, and is more than justified. When he stops at intervals, and goes in search of such passages, the quotation is then foreign to his thinking, it is a tag of embroidery stitched on the garment. It is said that there are ingenious books which contain extracts—very familiar, as a rule—on every religious subject, so that the minister, having finished his sermon on Faith or Hope, has only to take down this pepper-caster and flavour his somewhat bare sentences with literature. If this ignominious tale be founded on fact, and be not a scandal of the enemy, then the Protestant Church ought also to have an Index Expurgatorius, and its central authorities insert therein books which it is inexpedient for ministers to possess. In this class should be included 'The Garland of Quotations' and 'The Reservoir of Illustrations,' and it might be well if the chief of this important department should also give notice at fixed times that such and such anecdotes, having been worn threadbare, are now withdrawn from circulation. The cost of this office would be cheerfully defrayed by the laity.

Illustrations are of the last value to a sermon, because they both give colour to the style and interest to the thought, and the preacher ought to practise the art with diligence. One man will carry a subject for a week and never once detect an analogy in the life around him, because his mind is hermetically sealed. Another man will be overwhelmed by the wealth of analogy thrust on him from the books he reads, from scenes on the wayside, from the country during an hour's visit, from five minutes in a manufactory, from the sight of a vessel unloading, from a conversation overheard in a public conveyance; nature, life, commerce, literature, conspire to interpret his theme, till amid this embarrassment of riches he hardens his heart and grows fastidious. He is fortunate who can take his choice among competing illustrations till he finds one which brings out the exact point with felicity. It is for the preacher to decide how far he will labour his figure, which can be given either in a sentence or a page, and he will be guided by the composition of his congregation. One may lay it down as a rule that the details of an illustration should be in inverse proportion to the culture of the hearers. With uneducated people illustration has to be expanded into description, with educated it may be condensed into allusion. Upon alert and sensitive minds the speaker simply plays, as one touches the keys of a piano, when the note sounds without fail; but sluggish and callous minds he must galvanise by repeated shocks of electricity. Illustration is either panoramic or miniature painting, but, on the whole, must be on the larger rather than on the smaller scale. Whether it be description or allusion, the illustration is never to be used as a mere opportunity of displaying the speaker's eloquence or learning. It is not a pyrotechnic display before which a crowd stands in admiration, but a lamp by whose light the traveller finds his way along the dark street.

The fourth canon is *Humanity*. One has heard able and pious sermons which might as well have been preached in Mars, for any relation they had to our life and environment. They suggested the address a disembodied spirit might give to his brethren in the intermediate state, where it is alleged we shall exist without physical correspondence. This detached sermon is the only credible evidence for such an unimaginable state, but otherwise it does not appear effective. While the preacher should be very sparing with *I*, it ought to be possible for an expert to compose a biography of him from a year's sermons.

[If the minister desires to give a personal experience he can say 'one,' or 'a man,' and if his people suspect the identity it is no matter. They have been delivered from the perpetual 'I' which devastates some men's utterances, and from whose monotonous boom you never escape.]

If one live in the country he ought to master ploughing, and sowing, and harvesting; if he reside in a seaport, he ought to know the docks, with their strange cargoes and foreign vessels; if his work be in a manufacturing city, he ought to have learned the processes; and if his lot be cast in a fishing village, then it is a reflection on him should he not understand the sailing of a boat. The minister ought to be soaked in life; not that his sermons may never escape from local details, but rather that, being in contact with the life nearest him, he may state his gospel in terms of human experience. No doctrine of the Christian Faith is worth preserving which cannot be verified in daily life, and no doctrine will need to be defended when stated in human terms—above all, in the language of Home. The principle of vicarious sacrifice, for instance—that one person should get good from another's sufferings,—may be proved to be true by texts of Holy Scripture, and it may also be shown to be absurd by argument, but it may be placed beyond criticism by reference to a mother, through whose sufferings and self-denial the child lives and comes to strength. It was Jesus' felicitous manner to remove His Evangel from the sphere of abstract discussion, and to assert its reasonableness in the sphere of life. 'What man among you?' was His favourite plea. God does exactly what a man does or wants to do when he is at his best. The divinity of a sermon is in proportion to its humanity.

Our fifth canon is *Charity*, for surely if any form of human speech should be free from anger and bitterness it is a sermon. We may not deny that there is a time and use for invective, since we have all read the stern raillery with which the Prophets pursued idolaters. Perhaps the most perfect passage of sarcasm in literature is the forty-fourth chapter of Isaiah, and of denunciation the twenty-third chapter of St. Matthew's Gospel. There comes a time when carnal and ill-doing people must be punished; and the tongue is a fiery lash. Jesus had done His best to conciliate and win the Pharisees from their crooked ways, and now, in despair of their reformation, He lets loose His indignation. Doubtless, in His anger, as in His love, Jesus is our perfect example, but it is well for His disciples to remember that anger is much more risky than love. He is a poor creature who cannot be angry, and who is not ready to challenge wanton evil-doers. The thunderstorm has its function, but let it be brief, and be followed by the clear shining after rain. Sarcasm serves so little purpose, and does so much mischief, that it had better be left out of the preacher's medicine-chest. People cannot be turned from sin by gibes, nor scourged into the Kingdom of God by sneers. It seemeth to us, when we are still young, both clever and profitable to make a hearer ashamed of his sin by putting him in the pillory and pelting him with epithets. Such is the incurable perversity of human nature, that the man grows worse under the discipline, and even conceives an unconscionable dislike to the officer of justice. As we grow older and see more of life it seems easier to put a man out of conceit with his sin by showing him the winsome and perfect form of goodness. So full of surprises is human nature that he will loathe himself and be drawn to the preacher, and, best of all, love righteousness. He that scolds in the pulpit, or rails, only irritates; he that appreciates and persuades wins the day. No man is more heartily detested than a sarcastic minister. And let it not be thought that the rasping preacher is the alone faithful voice. Gentleness can be very severe, and he that has tact may say what he pleases. What people want, of every class and in every land, is comfort, and he that deals kindly then will have their hearts and their lives.

For our sixth canon we take *Delivery*, and here we touch on the vexed question of spoken *versus* read sermons. If it be fairly stated it is at once decided. It is

THE TECHNIQUE OF A SERMON

not whether a sermon ought to be prepared with the utmost ability of the minister, or whether he should say anything that occurs to him on the spur of the moment. Nor is it whether he had better write his sermon, or think it out carefully, and clothe his thought with words in the pulpit. And it is not whether some few men are not able to do both themselves and their thinking greater justice by reading what they have prepared to their people. The exact question is, whether, after the average man has studied his sermon, and done his best by it, he ought to read the result or say what is in him to his hearers face to face. The pew is unanimous in favour of delivery, and the pew is right.

[Here and there one meets a person who wishes that all ministers would read, but the explanation most likely is that his nervous system had been shattered by sitting under a minister who stammered, or collapsed at critical passages.]

No one outside the pulpit ever attempts to influence a popular audience from a paper, and he who makes the attempt from the pulpit suffers gratuitous loss. He does not gather the encouragement of the people's faces, and they miss the appeal of his eyes. He is not able to utilise every puff of wind in the sensitive atmosphere, as one can who holds the rope of his sail in one hand and has his other hand on the helm—alert and watchful. He can catch no happy inspiration: he can avoid no unexpected disaster: he can turn aside to no pleasant bay, but must go straight ahead.

An audience creates an atmosphere which, after a little experience, one can feel with such accuracy that he knows when they are with him or against him. Audience and speaker act and react on one another, so that a supercilious and frigid people can chill the most fiery soul,

THE TECHNIQUE OF A SERMON

while a hundred warm-hearted folk can make a plain man eloquent.

The reader has his own advantages, for he could preach his sermon to fifty people in a church holding fifteen hundred, or even address his peroration to a deaf and dumb asylum: the speaker has his disadvantages, for he must reckon upon an occasional break-down, and he cannot hope to preserve such finish of style as might be found in his manuscript. It may indeed be admitted that speaking is an act of sacrifice in which the preacher gains nothing for himself and may lose much, but in that self-mortification, by which the message gains and he loses, his strength may be found.

The last and greatest canon of speaking is *Intensity*, and it will be freely granted that the want of present-day preaching is spiritual passion. Of intellectual and social passion there is enough in the pulpit, and one has even been amazed at the most

THE CURE OF SOULS

strange of all enthusiasms, critical passion, when a preacher has become quite hot over the authorship of the Pentateuch. What is wanting, and what cannot be wanted, is the sense of the unseen and eternal—of the everlasting love of God, the atoning sacrifice of our Lord Jesus Christ, the unspeakable value of a single soul, the infinite pathos of human life, the tenderness of the Holy Ghost, and the graciousness of the Evangel. Bathed in such springs of profound emotion, no man will be able to preach without tears, which will be all the more affecting if they be in the heart rather than in the eyes. He will need no tricks of acting, for through his broken accents will be heard the voice of God, and he himself will slip out of sight and be forgotten, like the unknown monk who in a European cathedral drops the curtain from a sacred picture and leaves his charge face to face with the Crucified.

PROBLEMS OF PREACHING

CHAPTER III

PROBLEMS OF PREACHING

It is useful to devote a section of one's working library to Christian Biography, both ancient and modern, and to reinforce it carefully from time to time. We may not gain much inspiration in thinking, or much guidance in working, because the conditions of thought and service are so different; but this reading acts as a flywheel in our feverish religious life, in checking hasty impulses and saving us from fits of depression. There are moments, however, when the calmness and regularity of the worthies of last generation drive us to despair, as when one reads from the diary of the Rev. Joseph Tomlinson, in the memorial volume issued after his death, and much valued by his congregation :—

'*December* 10 (*Monday*).—Rose at 5.30, although tempted to remain in bed owing to the darkness and cold. Completed the first head of my seventh sermon in the course on Sanctification before breakfast. Have now sermons prepared for the next three months, and note with thankfulness that I can produce three sheets hourly without fail.'

The good man died in the fifties, at the age of eighty-six, having preached till ten days before his death, and never having been once out of his pulpit through sickness; and one has a distinct vision of him moving about with great authority and dignity among his people, and a vague recollection of his thundering in a sermon against those who denied creation in six literal days,—' which showed to what a height of insolent audacity infidelity was rising in those days.'

This early rising, which is a marked

feature in such biographies, and a needless irritation unto the generations following—this turning out of sermons by machinery, in longhand-writing without an erasure, and sometimes on pink paper—this immunity from perplexing questions—this infallibility in doctrine, as well as the fixed, smooth, untroubled face at the beginning of the book, suggest an atmosphere very different from that in which we think and labour.

There is a sense in which preaching must be the same in all ages, dealing as it does with the everlasting Evangel of the Divine Love. There is a sense in which preaching must differ with every age, addressed as it ought to be to the changing conditions of life and thought. Christ is not one, but many; and therein He has proved Himself the Son of Man and the Saviour of the world. There is the Eternal Spirit, which is the Spirit of God, and there is the Time spirit, which is the spirit of man. He who feels the breath of the human spirit only is a secularist—there are such, although they know it not, in the Christian pulpit,—and he who feels the breath of the Divine Spirit only is an ascetic. It is best when the soul lies open to both influences, for so the preacher is in touch with God and man, a go-between and mediator.

It ought to be frankly recognised that preaching is a much harder task for us than it was for our fathers. The critical spirit was not then abroad, but was confined to students' rooms. Neither accepted rules of Christian living nor fundamental doctrines of Christian faith were questioned. Controversy had only to do with ecclesiastical affairs or conflicting theories of orthodoxy. Preaching moved in an atmosphere of social conventionality and religious authority, when people knew what to expect and the minister said what was expected. The channel was well buoyed and lit, and the vessel never went beyond the bar, so that the river-trips were quite safe and uneventful. To-day a religious teacher makes for the open sea, and people feel in every sermon the swell of the Atlantic. It is an exhilarating and invigorating experience, but has its hazards for hearers and its anxieties for the preacher. Never could there have been any time when he required to be so fearless and honest, and at the same time so reverent and careful. When a man carries his own life and the lives of others in his hand, he may well pray for humility and the mind of Christ. One very practical question is, how far the preacher is to forget his own *individuality*, or how far he must subordinate it to the general claims of truth. It may be contended, with some show of reason, that a teacher of Christianity is bound, in the discharge of his duty, to expound every doctrine of the faith in order, and to explain the various experiences of the soul—as a professor of physics must take his students through statics and dynamics, although his own preference may be for heat or light. On the other hand, it is ever to be remembered that the atmospheric conditions of science and religion are different, and that a minister cannot teach doctrines with which he has no affinity, or moods through which he has never passed.

What may be called the universal theory of preaching used to obtain, and still lies as a burden on many ministers. None can tell, except those who have gone through the purgatory, what it was for one man to hammer out, bit by bit, a sermon on Justification by Faith, while he longed to be in the Sermon on the Mount; or for another to struggle with a Beatitude which was ever eluding the doctrinal net, while he would fain have been revelling in the early chapters of the Roman Epistle. Ministers are still living, and not yet on the retired list, who can recall the time when the following was the prescription for a sermon :—

Recipe
    Tinct. Hodgii   . . oz. j
    Aquæ ad   . . . oz. vj
        Misce et signetur.
One table-spoonful morning and afternoon.

The colouring material might vary with the communion, but the principle of the composition would be the same. Any variation on this formula was regarded with suspicion as theological quackery, and condemned by authorities. One result of this régime was to utterly dishearten some young ministers, and move them to abandon their life-work in despair. What happened in one case must have happened in many, but it is hoped will soon be incredible. A lad goes from a theological college, who has not yet found his métier, and has never preached a sermon. What his message may be neither he nor any man can tell, but he is quivering with ideas and dreams. He is appointed assistant in a city church, and counts himself fortunate because the minister is distinguished for personal piety and devoted service in the Evangel. From time to time he has to preach, and under the direction and example of his chief he takes in turn the classical texts of the evangelical faith, to find that they do not hold him, and that he does not hold the people. He has searchings of heart and gloomy forebodings. Is any man fit to be a messenger of Christ who can be dull, commonplace, 'feckless,' on 'Behold the Lamb of God, Who taketh away the sin of the world'?

One week he goes afield, and comes on the raising of the widow's son, and instantly catches fire. He creates the situation in his heart, and cannot rest till he has committed to paper the emotions that possess and master him. A year ago he had lost his mother. On Sunday he enters the pulpit charged with power, and with his first sentence the people are welded to him in a common sympathy. His subject is an incident which cleanses, sweetens, inspires humanity, and he knows what it is to preach. Next morning he receives six letters—to the end of his life he well remembers that budget: one is from a mother whose son has been spared through a dangerous illness, to say he had expressed her thankfulness; one is from a mother whose son died, to tell him that he has convinced her of the sympathy of Jesus—both women want to see him; one is from a son whose mother is dead, and who counts her life the means of his salvation—he thought she was in church with him; one is from a son who has sinned against his mother, and he is going home to see her that day—both men will drop in to see him if he doesn't mind. All four will have a question to ask—How did he know? The two other letters are anonymous. One from 'a well-wisher,' anxious to know how any minister can reconcile it with his conscience to offer hungry souls empty sentiment instead of bread; and the other from 'a simple Christian,' complaining that no reference has been made to conversion, which the writer points out is the vital point in the story of the widow's son. Both letters state that the sermon has given much dissatisfaction to the congregation. Had he been ten years older he would have put the two letters in the fire without a thought, and the four in his desk, to cheer him when he was weary. Four letters were positive—testifying to good received: they value 250 marks each; two letters were negative—testifying to no good received: they value 0. If so many people have been cured, it is of no importance that so many more people criticise the medicine. The testimony of one man, that he was blind and now saw, obliterates the opposition of the Pharisees who insist on *a priori* grounds that Jesus could not have opened the man's eyes. But this lad, more impressed than he will be later in life by 'well-wishers' and 'simple Christians,' consults his chief; and he, being of the old conventional school, and having possibly missed the appeal to two classes, is shaken, and thinks there was a 'want.' He advises that, whatever may be the subject, the Gospel should be brought in at some point, and by the Gospel he means the 'plan of salvation.' Nor is the good man requiring what he does not practise, for it was his glory to have found the doctrine of the Holy Trinity in the Book of Esther and the Atonement in Ecclesiastes, and it ought to be added that the people were edified by both discoveries.

The beginner now understands that he is at liberty to deal with any subject—

character, intellect, or duty—if he has an evangelical conclusion. His next sermon is on David and Jonathan, and his eulogium on an unselfish and heroic friendship moves the congregation visibly; but when, in fidelity to his instructions, he explains at the close that David is Christ and Jonathan the sinner, he feels his power depart from him instantly, and even the spiritual do not sustain him with any enthusiasm. An audience has a sensitive ear, and detects the transition from reality to unreality without fail. He therefore has to decide between preaching what he ought or what he desires, and in such circumstances he had better preach according to his bent, without fear or reserve.

Because a man must fulfil himself, and if God has made him St. James he must not nullify himself by attempting to be St. Paul. Wings suggest the air and fins the water, and although there be amphibious animals, yet one prefers to see a swan on a lake rather than on the dry land. We are bound to credit Providence with some intelligence of design, and if the Bible has an immense variety of truths, and the human mind an immense variety of gifts, then it is reasonable to conclude that there may be some correspondence between the message and the messenger. For some time the man may stumble about in search of his line, but one day he will strike it, as when the wheels of a car that has been wandering hither and thither, with great discomfort to the passengers, slip into the grooves.

It is not at all to be feared that the preacher who confines himself to his own message will fail to preach Christ. Some one has said that there is a road from every text to Christ, and this saying is true; but it has two applications, either that the preacher should start from the text on a pilgrimage to Christ, or that he should so deal with his text that Christ shall come and dwell in it. Is it not known to all that one may cry 'Lord, Lord' without ceasing and yet Christ be a stranger, and that another may not mention His name and the fragrance of Christ's garments be felt in the place? There are those who can so deal with the sacrifice of the Lord as make us think of a work, not a person, and those who can so plead for almsgiving as to bring us face to face with Him Who knew not where to lay His head. The evangelical character of a sermon does not depend on its subject, but on its tone, for whether the theme be taken from Proverbs or St. John's Gospel the sermon of a Christian preacher should live and move and have its being in the Lord. Wherefore let a man preach on any text between Genesis and Revelation with great freedom, if so be that he abide in Christ.

The second problem is *Popularity:* how far the servant of the Master is to lay himself out to attract an audience, and what expedients he is entitled to adopt. We have lived to see the relation between preacher and hearer reversed. In the past a congregation was obliged to listen to their minister twice on Sunday, although he bored them nigh unto death: they 'sat under him,' to use one of the most pathetic phrases in religious speech. In the present a congregation will attend once if they like the preaching, and otherwise will read magazines at home. The people used to fill the pews to please the minister, who very soon called to learn the cause of their absence. Now the preacher is apt to go to the pulpit to please the people, who will brook no dictation at his hands. There was a day when the preacher could break out in terrifying language on his hearers for sleeping, inattention, and such like faults. People are too intelligent and well-bred now to commit such breaches of good taste: they sleep at home. The day has come when the hearers estimate the preacher as if he were a singer, declaring him to be 'in good form,' or 'a little flat.' The one indispensable quality of the former sermon was soundness—of the contemporary sermon that it be interesting. If the speaker has a light touch and a graceful manner, if he be bright and vivacious, above all, if he be never tiresome, then he will be approved. The age works and lives at high pressure for six days, and on the seventh reposes to be wearied afresh; and just as it has the 'new' journalism with its paragraphs, and the 'new' magazines with their short piquant stories, for leisure moments of the week, the age requires the 'new' sermon for Sunday.

One does not of course blame the age because it insists on a living sermon, but one does blame the preacher who discredits the noblest themes by dulness. There are two men who astonish us: one who has almost nothing to give, yet serves up his morsel so daintily, and another who, having so much, offers it so coarsely. Perhaps the hearer nowadays has grown into an intellectual *bon vivant;* but good cooking is very appetising, and the cook has earned some reward. Perhaps one ought, as we were told in childhood, to be able to eat anything, but it requires a very strong stomach to face half-raw meat. Some strong men, both in learning and piety, really do all that is possible to alienate an audience by their style and manner, and they can have no complaint because they are passed by and left alone. It need not be because they are solid: it may be because they are uncouth. For there are certain concessions, besides an easy style, that even the most scholarly and rigid preacher may make to this generation without any loss of self-respect. One is to choose an attractive title for his sermon, and announce it before the text.

A title is a happy device, for it lets the people know the subject, and saves them from weary guessing through a historical introduction, and it gives them a measure by which to check the speaker's relevancy. Another is to acquire the art of elocution, which really is not born with us, but takes much learning. When a person says that he likes a speaker, he as often simply means that he has heard him, and it is not amazing the finest passages lose their force when every third word is inaudible. And a third quite pardonable expedient is to arrange related sermons in sets or 'courses,' because the development and sequence of the subject sustains the interest and gives a fillip to appetite.

[Four, or at most six, sermons are sufficient for one set: the people lose heart at the prospect of twelve on 'St. Paul's Idea of Faith,' or sixteen on 'Job.' Discretion has to be used in the title. I could not personally recommend one mentioned to me by a pious minister, 'The Limbs of the Almighty,' although he assured me that it had enabled him to include some strange texts, and that it had been much blest.] Above all must the speaker of to-day be clear, terse, forcible; in a word, real, without cant or superfluity—a good leader-writer on religion.

Certain expedients are, however, to be deprecated, and ought to be shunned like sin. One is wilful eccentricity, wherein a preacher without wit or genius, or force or earnestness, outrages every canon of good manners in the pulpit in order to tickle the groundlings and secure a crowd. Another is vulgar anecdotage about himself or his family or his experiences,—enforced by gross personalities. Another is sensationalism of subject, wherein a teacher, leaving the Evangel of Christ, lives upon the crimes of the week, hunting the columns of the evening papers for some heading which will gather a mob and a collection. The excuse which such charlatans offer for this travesty of preaching is the number of people gathered within hearing of the Gospel, but they ought to know perfectly well that no Gospel is heard and no good done. A congregation fed on this highly spiced food will relish nothing good or wholesome, but will ever demand hotter and fiercer condiments, till at last the preacher can no longer stimulate the debauched palate, and is deserted. Against religious sensationalism, *outré* sayings, startling advertisements, profane words and irreverent prayers, the younger ministry must make an unflinching stand, for the sake of the Church and the world, for the sake of our profession and ourselves.

Another problem is *Secularity*, and on it there may be considerable difference of opinion among equally honest and religious men. Ought a preacher, as a rule, to keep within the subjects which were the burden of Christ, or ought he to take considerable latitude in dealing with the affairs of the day? It is a very practical question, and since it embraces a wide range of instances, politics may be taken as a test case. Suppose it be assumed that every minister is also a patriot, and devoted to the commonwealth, is it his part to discuss politics in the pulpit, or, while retaining his personal convictions, and giving them effect by his own vote, is it for him to be absolutely neutral in public speech? On the one side it can be urged with much force that when a man becomes a minister he ought not to forego one privilege or fail in one duty of citizenship; that, as a leader of men, he ought to guide his people in this high affair; that politics, of all departments, needs the presence and influence of clean-handed, single-hearted men; and that, whatever be the case with the Church, the Kingdom of God has to do with the whole life of the community. The conclusion therefore is that a minister ought to be in the very thick of politics.

On the other side it may be pleaded that it is hardly possible for a minister to take any share in politics without being involved in the doubtful compromises and manœuvres to which all parties are inclined; that his habits of thought and lines of study to a large extent incapacitate him for practical politics; that, while there are exceptions, most ministers who have become politicians have lost in spirituality and failed in their own work; that the abstention of one class from active government, for certain good reasons, may be a strength, and cannot be any appreciable weakness, to the State; and that Jesus, although devoted to His nation, and living in very trying circumstances, kept Himself markedly aloof from the politics of His day. And now one reasons that the ministers had better follow the example of the Lord and the Apostles.

If he be himself led to this idea of his duty he will reap one singular advantage. It will be allowed him, as one secluded from the strife of parties, and as one against whom no charge of partiality can be brought, to inspire his people from time to time with the principles of righteousness which lie behind all measures, with the glorious traditions of the past, in which the whole nation shares, with the passion for the country's good which ought to stir every one of her children, with that feeling of brotherhood which welds all classes into unity. He will stand between jealous interests and contending parties as a mediator making peace, as a prophet leading into the paths of righteousness.

Our next problem touches the modern outlook upon human history which has been given to the Church in our day, and may be called *Solidarity*. In our boyhood the Gospel was understood to deal with the individual, now it addresses itself to the mass. Religion once consisted in saving one's self, now it stands in saving your neighbour. Christianity once was satisfied with a healthy soul, it has begun to demand healthy houses. Preaching concerned itself with the spiritual experiences of penitence, faith, forgiveness, holiness; it has travelled to-day into questions of capital and wages, international arbitration, reorganisation of society, and the improvement of living. It is not now the individual but the race who is before the preacher.

Two absolutely different sermons, with not one point of contact save Christ, could be preached to-day by an individualist of the old school and a solidarist of the new, from the text, 'Come unto Me, all ye who labour and are heavy laden.' One would treat of a person's weary conscience, the other of the multitude's weary life. The criticism on the former would be, 'Is he living in the present world?' on the latter, 'Does he believe that there is a world to come?'

When tides meet there is broken water, and many are tossed in their minds as to whether the pulpit ought to give its strength to the regeneration of the individual or of society. Certainly it were a departure from the method of our Lord to ignore the soul, with its awful responsibilities and immense possibilities, to starve the inner life, which is the spring of all good thinking and working, to be silent regarding the things unseen and eternal. Suppose by the insistence of the Church it could be brought to pass—which is a vain expectation—that every man should, in any measurable period of time, be well fed and dressed and housed, should be free from disease, idleness, weariness, should have equal rights, privileges, opportunities with his neighbour, then this bread-and-butter paradise were a poor exchange for the Eternal Hope. It is right to say that the Church must labour to bring heaven here, but this heaven is long of coming, and meanwhile the Church must comfort the oppressed, the suffering, the beaten in this present battle, with the vision of the City of Rest, where is no more pain, neither crying, for the former things have passed away. A policy of sanitation is excellent, but it cannot replace the Way of Salvation.

Christ's minister must, at the same time, remember that he is the representative of the Carpenter of Nazareth, Who had a very tender compassion for the proletariat, and by this Spirit has led them all those years through the wilderness to the borders of the Promised Land, and that he is the legitimate successor of those Hebrew Prophets who were the champions of the poor and the uncompromising enemies of tyrannical wealth. It is not for him to stir up strife between classes, but to make peace, yet if in any critical conflict between the poor and the rich the minister of Jesus sides with the strongest, then hath he broken his commission, and forsaken his Master. If the Church of the Nazarene lift not up her voice on behalf of those who 'labour and are heavy laden,' and is not a refuge for the poor and friendless, what good is she on the face of the earth? Nor must Christ's evangelist forget that a man hath a body as well as a soul, and that if the body be famished for want of the meat which perisheth, his soul may not be able to receive the Bread of Life, and that it is all very well to exhibit the excellent glory of the Christian life, but the hearers may happen to live in houses where it is physically impossible to be a Christian.

The Spirit of our Master is with us and is giving a wider range to the Evangel. We are being taught that Jesus did not die for individuals but for the race, and that the race must be embraced in the service of the Church; that the great social movements of every civilised nation in the direction of physical well-being, are not mere outbreaks of ungodliness and anarchy, to be preached at and shot down, but the will of God, Who is the Father of the East end as much as of the West, and whose good gifts belong to all His children; that the Incarnation of our Lord Jesus Christ contains a wealth of blessing for humanity which is only beginning to be revealed, and constitutes the one stable and fruitful bond of brotherhood; and that in the Risen Lord lies the power for the redemption and glorification of human life.

A fifth and very acute problem arises from the critical spirit which has been affecting the ministry for at least five-and-twenty years, and perhaps the time has come for describing it as the problem of *Pedantry*. Is it expedient, in the sense of being useful to an ordinary congregation, and is it necessary, in the sense of being incumbent on a minister's conscience, to unload upon the people his studies in Biblical criticism? It is quite open for a minister to say, 'My people have certain ideas regarding the literary construction of the Bible which are quite exploded, and I have at my disposal information which would illuminate the whole circumstances of the Book. If I withhold this knowledge for any reason—especially through the fear of man—then I do injustice to myself, who have failed in my duty as a teacher, and to my pupils, who might in after years reproach me bitterly.' So this faithful student prepares a course on the composition of the Pentateuch and another on the non-Davidic authorship of the Psalms, with many a careful little excursus into literary details in ordinary sermons.

Another minister, and let it be granted that he is perfectly honest also, takes up an opposite position. 'What do my congregation, being practical people, care about the date and authorship of the books of the Bible, if they can obtain the spiritual kernel contained in such husks? And as for myself, until the higher critics agree among themselves and give us facts, I propose to leave their speculations severely alone.' Then this preacher treats each portion of Scripture either in complete independence of environment, or in a setting of baseless traditions; and he will delight a certain type of hearers by occasionally making contemptuous references to critics and all their works.

After this pleading from opposite sides, one arrives at the following conclusions:—

(*a*) That while many of its theories have been discredited, or are doubtful, criticism has made a large and solid contribution to our knowledge of the Bible.

(*b*) That the Church ought to be most thankful to those pious and learned men who have laboured at great cost, not only of time, but also of comfort and reputation, in this department of sacred letters.

(*c*) That for any teacher of the Bible to ignore or disparage the reliable, or even probable, results of criticism, and not to give them to his people, is a serious neglect of duty.

(*d*) That to instruct an average congregation in the details of Biblical criticism would be tiresome and irritating, as well as arid and unedifying to the last degree.

(*e*) That an occasional lecture on some misunderstood book, say the prophecy of Jonah—which is the vindication of charity, —or on the Song of Songs—which is the glorification of holy love,—will always command interest by its elevation above details and its living humanity.

(*f*) That careful and systematic instruction in the literary and historical circumstances of the Bible is best given in classes to be conducted by the minister, and where the pupils can have the full benefit of his knowledge.

(*g*) That a minister, while pursuing his studies in this department with all diligence, must lay it to heart that the critical atmosphere is cold, and is apt to chill the Gospel; and that he has certainly made no gain, but a great loss, who can prove the existence of a second Isaiah, but has lost the tender piety of his fifty-third chapter.

What is wanted above everything to-day is positive preaching, by men who believe with all their mind and heart in Jesus Christ. If a man has any doubt about Christ he must on no account be His minister; and if one in the ministry be afflicted from time to time by failures of faith, let him consume his own smoke and keep a brave face in the pulpit. The pulpit is not the place for discussing systems of scepticism, or proving the instinctive truths of religion, or adjusting the speculative difficulties of Christianity, or apologising for Christ. Those are belated tactics.

For years the Church has been on her defence, meeting attacks from science, from philosophy, from literature, from history. We render thanks to God for the apologists of the faith who have done their work nobly with skill and nerve. They have held the ground with stubborn courage: it is now time for the cavalry to charge and complete the victory. We have defended and explained our Lord long enough; let us now proclaim Him, and magnify His Cross with a high heart and an unshaken voice in face of the whole world.

THEOLOGY THE THEORY OF RELIGION

CHAPTER IV

THEOLOGY THE THEORY OF RELIGION

Various questions must occur to his mind as a student leaves the theological college and enters on the work of the holy ministry; and this is not the least important, What am I to do with my theology? Am I to regard it as so much deck cargo which I shall jettison as soon as the ship puts to sea, or as the ballast which steadies the vessel in stormy weather? It will depend on the answer whether one continues the study of this great science as a matter of love, and remains a student of theology to the last day of his ministry, or abandons it as an instrument which has done its work and can be replaced by some other intellectual whetstone, say literature or social economy. Upon the face of it one must regret a wanton waste of time and labour, if the fruits of three years' hard study are flung aside, and do not become a capital of knowledge to be laid out at usury in the practical work of the pulpit. Is theology a merely academic science, or has theology a hold upon the mind of every thinking person? Must theology be confined to a man's study, or can it be taught in the market-place with our highest enthusiasm?

Unfortunately there are two schools which are much in evidence, and which, for different reasons, deprecate theology. One is the extreme left of the Christian Church, whom we may call the Rationalistic school—that body of superior persons who are understood to have the monopoly of religious culture, and are accustomed to regard the average Christian as a religious Philistine. With them the Catholic creeds are simply antiquarian documents,

THE THEORY OF RELIGION

which are outside criticism and demand very gentle handling. One of course uses different standards to try folklore and philosophy. The great Christian doctrines, so slowly and carefully created, have, in the opinion of this school, no more vitality than a fossil of the carboniferous period, and are of no more use than a battle-axe. Theology is a dead science, which is disappearing before the advance of education, along with astrology and the black art. It will be replaced by ethics and sociology, when religion is reduced to 'morality touched by emotion,' and the Church of Christ is a Society for the cultivation of æsthetics. St. Augustine must give place to Marcus Aurelius, and Calvin retire in favour of Comte. Do not disgust intelligent people with metaphysical speculations; better adhere to questions of daily duty, and for a relief take up 'a living wage' and the lives of the poets. Really there is no subject this school is not discussing in the pulpit, from Dante to Ibsen, from Home Rule to Bimetallism, with one severe and consistent exception, and that is the master themes which have engaged the intellect and stirred the heart of the Christian Church for nineteen centuries.

Theology is quite as distasteful to the extreme right of the Church, which regards religion and emotion as synonymous, and may be described as the Evangelistic school. [Distinguish between Evangelical and Evangelistic: the former is a generic word, the latter specific, the one covers a country, the latter defines a province.] Their objection is not that our science does not deserve the name, but that everything like ordered thinking is a foe to spiritual life. They regard with suspicion the idea that the Bible is a literature gradually evolved through the action of the Divine Spirit on the religious consciousness of a susceptible people, and bitterly resent the application of literary methods to its criticism. The Book is treated as if it had been given in a piece, and was perfect in every part, so that a doctrine can be proved with equal cogency by a text from Genesis or from the Gospels, and the very utterances of Jesus Himself have no supreme authority over those of Isaiah or St. Paul. It is perhaps inevitable that from a standpoint of such extreme simplicity this school should have little sympathy with any elaborate treatment of the facts of our faith, being quite convinced that the mystery of Christ's Sacrifice is made luminous beyond desire by some time-worn illustration of a person jumping into a boat or throwing himself from a burning house. When this spirited and excellent school is in a rampant mood, it is never weary of girding at theological education. We are reminded that the Prophets did not go to college— Jonah is sometimes put forward as an instance of a rapid and remarkable training,—and the suggestion is that any tincture of learning will be simply a rebate from fervour;—which is doing something less than justice to the culture of Joel, the oratory of the first Isaiah, the poetry of the second, the pathetic art of Jeremiah, or the amazing originality of the author of the book of Jonah. The Apostles are even used as an argument against a trained ministry, and uneducated men are held up as models for preachers, when Jesus Himself did not think that these chosen men were fit for their work until they had been three years under His constant care. Cannot any one see that St. John was a man of solitary genius, for whom there need be no rules? Can any one state in terms of University curriculum the value of those three years with Jesus? And at regular intervals some orator with an eye upon the groundlings makes the hackneyed contrast between learned men with-

THE THEORY OF RELIGION

out grace and unlearned men with grace—as if learning and grace were exclusive circles, and we were not all perfectly certain that there would not be a congregation left in the land within five years without the patient, unboasting labour of a trained and settled ministry.

[Our attitude to self-appointed religious speakers, and that of the medical profession to quacks, is a striking contrast. We, as a rule, welcome this assistance, in the public interest, and doctors will have none of it, also in the public interest. Both professions are quite unselfish. Which is in the long-run right?]

It is indeed a curious paradox that the left should sneer at theology because it is not worth understanding, and the right should condemn theology because it is past understanding, and so our unfortunate science be buffeted first on the one cheek and then on the other. But theologians may console themselves with the reflection that all this railing and girding at doctrine is simply one of the innumerable forms of modern cant, and that theology is an absolute intellectual necessity.

Whenever any student has collected a number of facts in his own department, whether his science be physical or metaphysical, he will be compelled by the laws of his mind to arrange his facts and discover their principle. Theology has exactly the same reason to exist as physics or psychology, with the additional advantage of an intense human interest. What is the genesis of a doctrine? Any doctrine of the first order is the answer to an imperative demand of reason; it is the best attainable explanation of a spiritual fact, historical or experimental. Why not rest in the fact without formulating anything? Because we are reasonable beings, and desire to give reason full play in the higher reaches of knowledge. Whenever the mind is awake, one asks questions concerning the why and the how of this fact. One examines the circumstances, and collects evidence, and sums up the results, and states the conclusion in a formula. Your formula is theology, and is the homage reason does to truth.

No one can hope to teach religion, in even its simplest form, with permanent success, without a competent knowledge of theology, any more than a physician can practise medicine without a knowledge of physiology, or an engineer build a bridge who has not learned mathematics. Without a system in the background of his mind, a preacher's ideas will have no intellectual connection or artistic proportion. Without a system underlying his sermons he cannot grip and impress his hearers. His own creed, instead of being a microcosm, will be a chaos, and his sermons between January and December will not be a picture growing to perfection of perspective and form, but a kaleidoscope of whirling and amazing colours. This type of preacher may have an audience enthusiastic and admiring, but he has no pupils on whom he stamps the lines of truth. You cannot trace him in the children of his teaching, because the likeness is so variable, just as the fashion of his own countenance was never two weeks the same. To-day he contradicts what he said yesterday :—but he is not inconsistent, he is only incoherent. Having no compass of thought he is carried away by fancies and speculations in all directions, making many stormy voyages, and sometimes, without doubt, coming home with good merchandise.

[One must distinguish between the teacher who affirms and denies the same thing, like an equation where the plus and minus signs are equal, and the result is $x=0$, and a teacher who gives in turn opposite poles of the same truth, and whose world of thought is rounded and solid.]

From the unsystematic thinker people may get inspiration—which is a great gain; they cannot hope for exposition. Of course a system in its bare outlines is unsightly and repulsive, and people have complained, with fair reason, of the dry bones of doctrine. An uncovered skeleton is certainly a very unlovely object, and defies the art of speech, but it lies behind the rounded grace of Venus de Medici, and alone sustains the weight of language. How far the closely knit and symmetrical form ought to appear through the flesh and blood may be matter of taste, there being, so to say, masculine and feminine contours of thought, but luxuriance and winsomeness must rest on strength. When people congratulate themselves because a sermon has been clear, it really means that it has been theological; and this may be true, although there be not one word of theology in it from beginning to end. The vine hid the trellis-work.

Theology has had wild speculations and many eccentricities, like every other science, but her master efforts, by which she must be judged, are strenuous attempts of reason to grasp the principles which are behind the phenomena of religion. It is open to urge that doctrines have grown antiquated and need to be recast: it is absurd to deny the necessity or utility of theology, as it is most unfair to ignore or disparage the remarkable ability which has gone to the creation of this science, and which was, in the catastrophe of the Roman Empire, the salvation of letters. They are unworthy of their profession who join in the Philistine outcry against theology, and allow it to be spoken of as something not worthy of serious study. If it be praiseworthy to classify beetles, and specialists among the coleoptera speak solemnly of their subject, it may be allowed for one science to reason regarding God and the soul. One can hardly imagine a greater sin against light within the Church than any indifference or enmity towards theology, or a more flagrant outrage against the idea of a University than the omission or exclusion of one science alone, and that the queen of all, and the one in which all others cohere and are crowned.

We are all apt, as preachers, to be browbeaten and reduced to silence by the impudent assertion that an average audience has no interest in theology, and will only listen to us upon the astounding condition that we do not give them the one thing we are supposed to have thoroughly learned. They expect from a historian history, from a geologist geology, but from a teacher of theology—and we are the only teachers of theology for the public—

anything, however remote from the subject, provided it be neither very solid nor thoughtful. May I suggest that the dumb public is often libelled by blatant spokesmen, and means to say something different. Examine the literature which finds favour with the people, and it would not occur to you that the people dislike theology. Within the last few years, for instance, four works of fiction have excited great attention, and been read on every hand. One is *John Inglesant*, which contains a better account of Quietism than you will find anywhere outside Alfred Vaughan's *Mystics*. The second is the *Story of an African Farm*, throwing a strange light on the wooden and unlovely theology of the Dutch Boers. The third is *John Ward, Preacher*, which is a powerful indictment of an extreme type of Calvinism which has in the past often paralysed the life and energy of the Presbyterian communion. The fourth is that remarkable and over-estimated book, *Robert Elsmere*, and every one knows that Mrs. Humphry Ward has been simply discussing, under the guise of fiction, the problem of historical Christianity, which is weighing heavily on many minds to-day. This school of fiction is a phenomenon, and, so far as one knows, is a new thing in letters. It is impossible to mistake its significance or to deny the desire it meets in the public mind. One may have his own opinion about the merits of the books. One may be doubtful about their taste. One may also view with apprehension the habit of popularising theology to the point of vulgarity, and wince when the resurrection of our Lord is discussed in drawing-rooms, and the miraculous decided between the soup and the fish. This is from the cloister to the market-place with a vengeance, and thoughtful people must have anxieties. Both Agnostics and Christians may desiderate the former reserve, and neither would like to have the veil utterly torn from the Holy of Holies in the soul. One may also be haunted by the conviction that the combination of fiction and theology may result in the decay of an art and the travesty of a science. But the trend of the graver intelligence among the public is evident, and it is distinctly towards those great questions which form the substance of the Christian faith, and lie at the foundation of religion. People will lie becalmed in morals, and even in physical science, weary unto death, but if any one dares to deal with questions of faith after an understanding fashion, he has the wind with him.

But my evidence on this point is not confined to a few phenomenal novels, which are now giving place to other works of pseudo fiction on the second burning question of the race—for there are only two—Love and Religion. Four books have lately appeared more or less powerfully to

THE THEORY OF RELIGION

the more serious public intelligence, and each has had a collateral connection with the problems of theology. One is Mr. Balfour's *Foundations of Belief;* another Mr. Pearson's *National Life and Character*, the prophecy of pessimism; the third, Mr. Kidd's *Social Evolution*, which is the first recognition, on scientific grounds, of religion as a factor in the development of society; and Professor Drummond's *Ascent of Man*, an attempt to evangelise Evolution. No leading review is considered complete without an unvarnished theological article, and its editor is happy if he can organise a controversy on the future state or a miracle of Jesus, enlisting as delighted contributors all kinds of people, from retired scientists to Ministers of the Crown. Draper's *History of the Conflict between Religion and Science* has gone through more editions than any other book of the International Science Series, and it would be interesting to know how

Lux Mundi compares in sale with any book on politics of the last ten years. If the pulpit be afraid of theology, the editors are not, and they are an infallible barometer of popular taste. The air is as theological to-day as in those early centuries when men settled the niceties of the Nicene Creed with their fists, and the religious world was divided into two camps by a diphthong.

Any one desiring to preach theology has an audience as large as that which waits on the physicists, but he can only hold it by fulfilling two conditions. The first is very reasonable—it is that he has mastered, or has at least a competent knowledge of, his science. Preachers have not always this qualification, and intelligent hearers have discovered that their teachers knew little more than themselves, and only led in dogmatism and declamation. We must recognise the fact that intellectual culture is being more widely diffused every year, and that a considerable proportion of the younger generation read theology. They are curious about the latest theory on the Song of Solomon; they are perfectly acquainted with the dual authorship of Isaiah; they have their doubts regarding the authenticity of Second Peter; they have tried to trace the documents of the Hexateuch. It may be a clerk in a town who has access to a library, or a schoolmaster in some college who has spent his spare cash in books. One must not presume on the ignorance of the most rustic people; there may be one reader in the little church, and there will be six soon. Others may wish to go into the question of orders, or the doctrine of the Sacraments, or the history of creeds, or the theory of the 'higher life.' It is the Renaissance of theology, with all the hopefulness and restlessness of a new movement. These amateur students will turn to us, and they have a right to expect our help. If it appears that after a careful training, and with a life consecrated to such study, we know less than the inquirers, they will not trouble us farther, but we shall be despised like a doctor who needs to be taught by his own patient. If, on the other hand, we are so far left to ourselves as to frown on such study and label it dangerous, then we shall be suspected of dishonesty. We must accept the age into which Providence has cast us, and enter into its spirit. One can hardly imagine any more honourable task than to meet its wants and to guide its inquiries. There are ages which have been saved from sin by evangelism; this is an age which must be saved from scepticism by knowledge.

One of course remembers the enormous extent of theology, and I am not suggesting that each minister be an original worker. The day was when one man would write a commentary on the whole Bible and all subjects therein, from its prophecies to its geography, but this were now a labour of Hercules. Theology, like every other science, has been divided into departments, and each has its own specialist. One takes Old Testament History, another Prophecy, a third the Gospels, a fourth the Epistles. There is dogma, exegesis, Church history, ethics, palæography. To-morrow there may be farther subdivision, until each book in the Bible, and each period in the history of the Church, and each doctrine of the faith has its master. We must accept the distinction between a professed scholar and a working minister, as we do between a consulting physician and a general practitioner. We are the general practitioners, who owe a debt of gratitude to the experts, and can best discharge it by using their work. Our sphere is that of theological middlemen, who will distribute among the public the selected and assorted produce of the schools. We must not only overtake the past, but also keep abreast of the present, using every spare moment to read and digest the latest and best theology, that our people may have the full benefit of that great revival of thought which is making the Bible to blossom like the rose.

It would be a happy enterprise for the Church to supplement the efforts of her working clergy by sending experts to lecture in the larger towns and, so far as possible, in country centres, on the chief themes of theology. This expedient would confer a double benefit, for it would rear a race of believing scholars and would convey the latest results of theological science to our people, untainted by that spirit of speculation which revels in baseless theories, and that insidious unbelief which quietly eliminates the supernatural. One would also like to see a series of theological handbooks, written by competent men and in a vigorous style, so that any man, learned or simple, in our land could secure as reliable and interesting information on theology as on physics or physiology. If men are now awaking to the claims of the queen of sciences, the credit can hardly be given to the Church, but if her children have to go to unbelieving scholars for satisfaction, the sin of such a disaster will lie at the Church's door.

The second condition of success is that we place our science before a cultured generation in a becoming dress. It is a shame when theology is more poorly clothed than comparative anatomy or political economy, and her savants cannot be acquitted of carelessness. They have been so anxious to secure light that they have been indifferent to sweetness. Anything more barbarous than the jargon of the Puritan theologians, with a few exceptions, can hardly be imagined. Owen is their most representative divine, and the most tedious and uncouth writer upon one's shelf. Yet the Puritans lived at the close of the Augustan period of English letters, when Shakespeare was just dead and Milton was writing *Paradise Lost*. It is one of the reproaches of Puritan thought, both former and latter, that while it has added enormously to theology, it has contributed only one book, *The Pilgrim's Progress*, and possibly Howe's *Living Temple*, to literature. The explanation certainly does not lie in any necessary divorce between culture and theology. Erasmus, the pioneer of modern theology, and that beautiful spirit, Sir Thomas More, both lovers of learning and children of faith, attempted an eirenicon. But almost immediately the theologians and the Humanists parted company, and since then the theologians, with some fine exceptions, have contemned letters, and the Humanists have had their merry jest at theology. But that is no

THE THEORY OF RELIGION

reason why words should not wait on the theologian like nimble servitors as readily as on the poet. He cannot indeed be a theologian unless he be also, in spirit, a poet; for poetry and Christianity live and move and have their being in the same region. Theology, after all, has had her stylists, and it is a liberal education to read her masters. The majesty of Hooker, the brilliance of Jeremy Taylor, the sweetness of Leighton, the purity of Newman, the incisive vigour of South, the aptness of Bushnell, and the force of that untrained theologian John Bunyan, are a delight and a model. Theology which has not been in the main current of letters is invariably stranded in some creek and forgotten; the men who added culture to science live and flourish. [Samuel Rutherford and Archbishop Leighton were of the same period—both fine scholars and finer saints. Rutherford's theology is unread, while Leighton's

St. Peter is on every theologian's shelf, because the one is literature and the other is not.] People will decline to taste theology barbarously served when Professor Huxley has been making natural science as fascinating as a romance. Letters take a swift revenge on the arrogant theologian by denying him their aid in his hour of need, and teaching him the useful lesson that there must be no separation between culture and religion.

It remains for each minister to decide how far he will give distinct instruction in theology to his people, but he has no alternative about leavening his preaching with theology. Just as the great masters in art used to paint the nude figure complete in every line and muscle before they draped it with garments for some Christ, so must the most accurate theology underlie every sermon, to secure it with intellectual consistency and to invest it with spiritual force. But when one has said his last word for the study of theology, there still remains for the Christian teacher another qualification, without which his theology will be vain, and, indeed, he cannot be a theologian. Between our science and every other there is this difference, that in other departments of knowledge one must know to love, in Christian theology one must love to know. In vain will be every place of learning, however thoroughly equipped, and any masters, however scholarly; in vain will be all books and study, if the soul have no spiritual vision. 'What availeth it to know the doctrine of the Holy Trinity,' says an ancient Father, 'if we have not humility?' He can understand truth whose mind has been illuminated by the Spirit of God and his heart cleansed by the Cross of Christ. It is good to use all the means of learning with diligence, but best to live in fellowship with Jesus, for he only who comes forth from the secret place of God will carry with him the Living Word and the Divine Unction.

THE NEW DOGMA

CHAPTER V

THE NEW DOGMA

EVERY student of Church history is aware that theological science has not developed along a straight line, but in a course of progressive and sometimes intersecting circles. Those circles differ in character, some completing themselves in a shorter period than others, or embracing a smaller province of the Church; but, as a rule, each has four segments, and by taking an observation one can tell where his age is in this evolution of thought.

There is the pre-doctrinal period, when truth is held in solution and has not yet crystallised. The Church has no doctrine regarding the Person of Christ, or His Sacrifice, or the Holy Trinity, or the history of man. The Christian simply believes in Christ, and lives with Him, and learns from Him, and follows Him unto death, because Christ has loosed the power of his sin, or comforted his sore heart, or fulfilled his spiritual aspirations, or cast light on the darkness of the grave. The Church is not yet self-conscious, nor has she realised her faith. Her position is, with St. Peter, 'Lord, unto Whom can we go but unto Thee? Thou hast the words of everlasting life.' This is the age of *Mysticism.*

Then comes the doctrinal period, when the truth is precipitated and takes its first visible form. Under the pressure of speculation, or on the attack of unbelief, the Church pauses in the current of her emotions and inquires what she believes.

[Whom she believes, she knows, and Him through every change of creed she ever believes, returning from her furthest

THE NEW DOGMA

journeys of theological science to His side.]

There is ample liberty of discussion, since there are no precedents for reference, no standards of authority. The traveller has no map of guidance, for the land has never been surveyed, although people have lived and rejoiced in its fatness. Slowly and painfully, with fierce intellectual tumult, and often with disgraceful commotions, the Church discovers her mind.

[One may never know what is in his mind till some one expresses it for him, hence our gratitude to a poet who makes us articulate.]

Consider how the most elaborate and complete doctrine of the Catholic Faith, the doctrine of our Lord's Person, was evolved from the consciousness of the Church. An acute and pious scholar denied the Deity of Christ, and the Church received a shock of surprise.

After keen discussion the Church, in Council assembled, declared that Christ was very God. But the question of our Lord's Person had now been made matter of debate, and reason must work it out to the end. Another ecclesiastic, as might be expected, now denied Christ's humanity, and the Church affirmed that He was true Man as well as true God. It almost followed, as reason sounded her way through this sublime mystery, that some one would in that case assert that Jesus must be two persons, and after deliberation the Church asserted the one person of Jesus. So it came to pass that a fourth theologian assumed one nature in Jesus, and once more the Church gathered and laid down the two natures of the Lord. After this fashion was the doctrine of Christ's person wrought out by valid and repeated processes of reason—an inevitable and orderly evolution—and the work of the four Councils remains unto this day. Instead of the individual Christian saying, 'I believe,' the Church meets and repeats the Nicene Creed. This is the age of *Dogmatism*.

Next follows the post-doctrinal period, which is not capable of exciting human interest, and is afflicted with an insufferable weariness. The doctrine which flowed molten from hearts fired with divine love has now run down into a mould and settled into a cast-iron shape. During this period scholars give themselves to the application of the doctrine in directions which were never intended by its author, and to the battle of details, most of which are of quite minor importance. The doctrine ceases to be a living reality, and becomes a mere intellectual proposition, which, if a man hold, he shall be saved, even though he be an open sinner; which, if he deny, he shall be damned, even though he be a radiant saint. This is the age of *Scholasticism*.

[It is good to remember that, however cold and detached from life any doctrine may seem to us in our day, it must once have expressed the profound conviction of believing Christians, and that the kernel contained in its husk is eternal. There is no doctrine of the first order which does not enshrine a living idea of religion.]

Lastly comes a time when earnest men, growing weary, not of the principles, but of their forms, propose to make a clean sweep of dogma. They raze the building to the ground, and then proceed to closely examine the foundations. The Church goes back again to the elementary facts of revelation and experience, to test their authenticity and reality, and to see what use can be made of them for the good of the individual soul and the common spiritual life. This spirit is not of necessity arbitrary or disloyal; it may be most pious and humble. Nor need it be iconoclastic:

doctrine may be tried only to be approved. This is the age of *Criticism.*

There is first the age of St. John, then the age of Athanasius, then the age of the schoolmen, then comes the age of Erasmus. After which another circle commences.

[Each period is to be found incarnate in contemporaneous Christians, and any large congregation can afford a mystic, a dogmatist, a schoolman, and a critic. Between one whose dogma is a living part of his soul, and another who carries his dogma like a pocket-game he can show on occasion, there is an enormous difference. If you attack the former, you wound him; if you attack the latter, he gets angry. One ought never to despair of a critic and count him hopelessly cold; he is conscious himself that he is in the arctic zone, and may set off for the tropics any day. When a critic changes he always becomes a mystic.]

THE CURE OF SOULS

It is not difficult to identify the age of our fathers, whose teachers we remember with veneration, but whose teaching is responsible for a revulsion in their children, which has often gone to dangerous and foolish extremes. They did not create dogma, throwing no new light on the supreme subjects of our creed; they were not critics, adding nothing to the sources of dogma. They received what had been created, and defended the deposit rigidly to its jots and tittles. They pursued doctrines into all their recesses and minutiæ, and cast saints out of the Church for differing from them on some sub-theory of a doctrine. Great and fruitful conceptions, like the Holy Trinity and the Incarnation, were isolated from life, and their ethical context never even suspected; and one recalls with a shudder how the one was treated like a problem of Euclid, and the other as a clever expedient. The idea of Inspiration was reduced to a mechanical theory, which made the divine origin of the Bible incredible, and the Church, in dearth of any great intellectual interest, gave herself to futile discussions regarding the lawfulness of hymns and organs in public worship. The night is darkest just before the dawn, and one knows when such things come to pass that scholasticism has reached its height in any Church, and that the day of criticism is at hand.

When in certain quarters of the Church intelligent Christians were in keen debate as to whether Christ died for all men or only for some, and whether He suffered our exact punishment or its equivalent, the spirit of criticism, which in Germany had long been dealing with classical literature, began to work on Holy Scripture. It was some time before the English-speaking Churches felt the effects of this new movement, but it is worth recalling that in 1841 Frederic Myers, the curate of St. John's Church, Keswick, published a volume entitled *Catholic Thoughts on the Bible and Theology*, in which he stated, in a very lucid and persuasive manner, the modern idea of the form of the Bible, and which is a veritable seed-plot of reasonable thought. For a quarter of a century at least, the intellectual resources of the Church have been withdrawn from the study of dogma (with, of course, some brilliant exceptions) and devoted to criticism, with the grateful result of adding a new and opulent district to theology, whose waters, fresh and overflowing, have irrigated and revived neighbouring provinces.

The ministers of to-day have been trained in this age and baptized into its spirit. We have shared the hopes and endeavours, we have felt the doubts and anxieties of our time, and we can now frankly tell our people its faults and fruits.

Criticism has offended the Church by its *pretentiousness*, for its preachers were apt to speak as if they had a new Gospel. Of course they had nothing, and could have nothing, of the kind. They have given a large amount of information and they have removed some traditions, but a message for the soul criticism can never offer. The Gospel is a certain voice of God, which sounds from the first book of the Bible to the last, and any science which handles the body of the books does not come near the soul. The critic has established a debt of gratitude at the hands of the Church, but when he confounds himself with the evangelist he has forgotten his place.

Criticism has also sinned through *uncharitableness;* for some of the pioneers of the new school have forgotten good manners, and have not carried themselves respectfully to the past. While a discoverer in physics is ever grateful for the work done by his predecessors, and corrects their mistakes with humility, recognising that he stands on their shoulders, and that his results will also one day be revised, the biblical critic has been inclined to treat the old scholarship with unconcealed contempt, and to expose its errors with malignant satisfaction. Criticism has been misunderstood and slandered, it has been persecuted and martyred, and in this treatment of her honest and faithful servants the Church has sinned ; but in her justification it may be freely urged that criticism has often had little regard for the feelings and beliefs of the older generation, which may have been obscurantist, but was also reverent and saintly.

[If a minister feels it his duty to advance any new view, his style of speech ought to be especially cautious and considerate, because he must give a shock to many good people, and is in danger of shaking the faith of some. When a liberal in theology is bitter and intolerant, it is a satire on his position, and any disaster which follows has been earned. One has the strong conviction that the advocacy of advanced opinions ought to be entrusted to men of large build and robust constitution. People will take from a big, good-natured man what would goad them into frenzy from a little man with a shrill voice.]

Criticism has, however, rendered two great services to the working ministry, and one is apologetical. Almost all the moral attacks upon the Bible, which may have been cheap, but which were very embarrassing, fall to the ground as soon as the Bible is seen to be a progressive and gradual revelation. When the massacre of the Canaanites, and certain proceedings of David are flung in the face of Christians, it is no longer necessary to fall back on evasions or special pleading. It can now be frankly admitted that, from our standpoint in this year of grace, such deeds were atrocious and that they could never be according to the mind of God, but that they must be judged by their date, and considered the defects of elementary moral processes. The Bible is vindicated because it is, on the whole, a steady ascent, and because it culminates in Christ.

Criticism has also handed the Bible to the working minister, re-arranged, re-edited, re-bound, and so in this way made it for his purpose a more intelligible and interesting book. When a prophet and his environment are adjusted, his speeches are re-issued with illustrations which have a very practical application to our day: when the Book of Ecclesiastes is referred to the days of the third century B. C. then its note is caught, and any man who has been wronged and embittered by political tyranny and social corruption has his bitter cry included in the Book of God. The Bible as it comes from the critics is more real, because it is more human; not a book dropped down from heaven, untouched with a feeling of our infirmities, but a book wrought out through the struggles, hopes, trials, victories of the soul of man in his quest after God.

One thing the minister must lay to his heart and impress on his people, and that is the perfect harmony between faith and criticism. Without any exception, the most reliable and brilliant scholars of our English-speaking communions have been, or are, believing and devout men, who rejoice to turn from the study of the literature to declare the Gospel of the Bible. It ought also to be pointed out, that the total results of criticism, when they converge upon a point, have been, not to obscure or belittle Christ, but rather, to throw Him into supreme relief Whom all the prophets anticipated, Whom the apostles declared. The most fearful or most unlearned Christian ought to be comforted and gladdened with the assurance that after criticism has practically finished her work, the faith of the Church is more firmly and reasonably established. It is the ministry who must explain this to the people, because the people have learned to accept their word, and because the critics have done so much for the ministry.

It is, however, evident that the force of criticism is nearly exhausted, and the signs are on every hand that we have already entered on an age of mysticism. The great devotional writers, A'Kempis, Tauler, Boehme, Law, and Andrews, have obtained a new hold on the religious mind: poets like Herbert and Keble share their popularity: and William Blake, the poet-painter, is now a cult. Pious people meet together in country places for conference on spiritual things, and while such conferences were once the repetition of Sunday sermons, they are now devoted to esoteric religion, where three classes are recognised, the unregenerate, the regenerate, and the perfect, who have received a

THE NEW DOGMA

baptism of the Holy Ghost and entered into the deeper secrets of the religious life.

[Conferences for the deepening of the spiritual life prove that many earnest Christians are dissatisfied with both dogma and criticism, and are longing for the inner light and direct communion. For religion has three places of abode—in the reason, which is Theology; in the conscience, which is Ethics; and in the heart, which is Quietism. One is bound to welcome such gatherings of the 'Friends of God' and wish them prosperity, but, at the same time, one cannot but feel regret that the Church has not supplied every want of her children; and one is sometimes a little disappointed that the new Quietists are so bound by the letter of Holy Scriptures, playing with words in a way that cometh near absurdity, and that they do not claim kindred with their lineal ancestors both of the days before and after the Reformation.

THE CURE OF SOULS

Our Quietists seem to be wandering round their home, but some day they will find the door, and enter in to possess their family inheritance. The minister ought to have a very tender care of such choice and tender souls in his congregation, holding private converse with them, and from time to time feeding them with food convenient from their favourite pastures of the Psalms and St. John's Gospel.]

The conclusive proof that we are already in the midst of a true and sane mysticism is the instinctive return to Christ, where on every side and from all schools Christian souls are making for their place of birth, as fish find again their native stream. Many traditions have been swept away, and many theories laid aside; but above the dust of controversy rises the face of Christ. Surely there has been no age since that early morn, when the echo of His footsteps was still on earth, and His very appearance in the flesh was remembered, wherein Christians have been so anxious to understand what Jesus was and what He taught. Nor has there been any age since the days of the Roman Martyrs where there has been such devotion to His person, whether you gather the evidence from the Salvation Army, which, with all its apparent extravagances, is touched with a noble and simple heroism; or the Missions, whose martyrs are taking possession of Africa for the Lord.

When a minister leads his people in the return to Christ, it is well for him to avoid two extremes. He must neither go to the Gospels alone, for there he is dealing with an earthly Christ, nor to the heavens alone, for then is he dealing with an unknown Christ, but to Him Who is alive for evermore, and Whom we have in the Gospels. Criticism gives us the historical Christ, and mysticism gives us the spiritual Christ, and both united give us the real Christ.

We ought to pray that the mystical spirit may long continue and make tender our hearts, but it is almost certain that the Church will soon begin the reconstruction of dogma, and that men are living who will have their share in the enterprise. Dogmatic theologians are still very rare, but the material is rapidly accumulating for their work, and the Church will soon demand that the results of the New Criticism and the new exegesis be gathered and stated in the form of doctrine. A few swallows herald the spring, and Dr. Fairbairn's *Christ in Modern Theology* and Canon Gore's *Incarnation* are the beginning of a time—a time for which many are praying.

If, however, the Christian Church of next century is to have beautiful and acceptable doctrine, then it can only be under two conditions that were not known

THE NEW DOGMA

in the past. One is, that theology be allowed the same liberty as any other science, mental or physical. Why is it dogma has excited so fierce a dislike that the mere suggestion of a revival of dogma fills many intelligent and liberal minds with dismay? It is not because they could deny to theology the same right to formulate her conclusions as physics, or that they could close their eyes to the immense progress theology has made within recent years. They remember that the Church was not content in the past to state her mind as to dogma, but insisted on making that dogma final, and binding it for ever on the faith of the members, and they are haunted by the fear that this sad tragedy may be repeated. Why is it that the physicist has no grudge at his predecessors and never girds at them, while the modern theologian is inclined to rend his fathers? The physicist has not been confined to the limits of the fourth or sixteenth centuries, while the dead hand of Councils and Confessions rest on the theologian. It is to be hoped that every branch of the Christian Church will soon exact no other pledge of her teachers than a declaration of faith in Jesus as the Son of God and the Saviour of the world, and a promise to keep His commandments, and otherwise grant to them the fullest freedom of thought and exposition.

The other condition is that the obvious distinction between religion and dogma be frankly recognised. One may walk in the light and know nothing of astronomy, as did St. Thomas, who was practically a slave of Jesus and doctrinally a sceptic concerning Christ. One may have studied astronomy and walk in darkness, as did the Pharisees, who were accomplished in doctrine and sent Jesus to the Cross. It is rather discreditable that a Christian should not think out the theory of his faith, and he should be exhorted and encouraged by his minister to take up theology, but to the end of the chapter there will be sound thinkers who are poor livers and erroneous thinkers who are splendid livers. Under such favouring circumstances theology will at last obtain her opportunity, and come into her kingdom.

When this age begins, we may hope to witness a remarkable revival of forgotten thought; and it will not, some dare to imagine, be so much a new theology as an old theology, which came before its time, that will at last be acclimatised in Christian faith. It is well known that there were two schools among the Fathers, the School of St. Augustine and the School of Clement of Alexandria. The one school rested all theology (speaking in a general but sufficiently exact sense) upon the conception of the Eternal which made Him a Law Giver and a Sovereign. The other school, that of Clement, rested the conception of the Eternal upon the idea of His Fatherhood. Many have been filled with wistful regret that Clement of Alexandria had not his due effect upon the thought of the Christian Church. But let us not reflect upon the Divine Spirit, nor come to rash conclusions on the development of doctrine. One can see very clearly that there is a relation between the moral state of the human race and its conception of the Deity. There is a growth in the idea of God in the experience of the individual, and in the experience of the race; and the full idea of God comes slowly to its height. No one can deny that the first thing that has to be lodged in the mind of the human race, especially when in a spiritually low and uneducated condition, is the idea of the Divine power and of the Divine holiness. That was especially necessary when the world was crumbling into pieces through corruption, and one can understand how the Christian theology stepped into the throne of a dead Roman Empire and ruled the consciences of men unto salvation, when one remembers that the doctrine of Augustine was bound upon the moral consciousness. The doctrine of Clement would have been premature and would have failed of ethical success. But his evangelical theology was not in vain; and now when we have got into our blood for ever the conception of God which crowns Him the King, Holy and Almighty, we are prepared upon a sound moral basis to receive Him as the loving and merciful Father. One therefore anticipates that the new doctrine will be based on the conception of the Divine Fatherhood—not the Fatherhood which throws away the Judgeship and the Righteousness of God, but the Fatherhood that gathers these up into a nobler and final unity; and that the Incarnation of our Lord Jesus Christ, as the revelation of the Father and the Head of the human race, will yield more blessed and practical fruit in the life of the race from year to year.

It must have been a great joy to breathe the air in the periods of Renaissance, whether in Physics or in Letters—to live in the days that preceded the Reformation, when classical scholarship was revived and placed again before the world: to live in the days of Elizabethan Letters and to feel the inspiration of Spenser and Shakespeare! Some of us know what it is to have seen the immense discoveries and bright hopefulness of physical science in the century; but there has been nothing in all these periods so glorious as the day when the theology of the Christian Church shall rise again, having lost nothing that was good and true in the past, and be reconstructed on the double foundation of the Divine Fatherhood and the Incarnation of our Lord Jesus Christ. We shall then see, I believe, an inspiring reconciliation, the greatest that can be made. We have often hoped for reconciliation between science and religion, where none is needed; often hoped for reconciliation between reason and faith, where none is needed, since each works in a different department of human life; but there is a reconciliation needed for which all devout and reverent men yearn, and it is the reconciliation between dogma and religion. They are not antagonistic, and if they have ever been forced into lamentable rivalry, they will make a covenant of peace in the love of the Father and of Jesus Christ His son.

One of the most suggestive pictures of Italian Art represents the meeting of St. Dominic and St. Francis. St. Dominic belonged to that order which was charged with the development and conservation of doctrine and who, on account of their theological bitterness and often unreasoning persecution, were called the 'hounds of the Lord.' St. Francis, as a great

THE CURE OF SOULS

French critic declared, was the most beautiful Christian character since the days of Jesus, and it was he who revived religion. In this picture St. Dominic, the author and defender of dogma, and St. Francis, the humble disciple and exemplifier of Jesus Christ, have met, and, flinging their arms round one another's necks, they kiss each other, so uniting what God had joined and no man ought to put asunder—the joyful religion of the soul and the reverent dogma of the intellect; a felicitous prophecy of the day when

> Mind and soul, according well,
> May make one music as before,
> But vaster.

THE MACHINERY OF A CONGREGATION

CHAPTER VI

THE MACHINERY OF A CONGREGATION

PERSONS living, and who may live for many years, can remember when the congregation was a very simple organism—a mere Bathybius of the ecclesiastical world. People attended two services on Sunday; the children went to Sunday-school; the minister had a class to prepare young people for their first sacrament. Congregations of the lighter kind indulged in a social meeting once a year, and those of a sterner cast adventured with a mission. The buildings, besides the church, consisted of a vestry, and, in some advanced cases, a hall under the church, low-roofed and dark, with, it might be, a couple of cellar rooms, where the young folk, returning to the primitive state of Christianity, met in dens and caves of the earth. Neither did the congregation involve itself in any public efforts for the regeneration of society, and would have been amazed had they been asked to take steps for the reduction of public-houses in the town, or to open an institute for the social and intellectual culture of the neighbouring district. Some enthusiastic people, pioneers of a coming day, carried on little enterprises of their own on week-days in the under ground premises — a Band of Hope or a sewing party; but such efforts were a mere by-play, and never passed into the main current of the congregational life. The duty of the minister was to prepare his sermons for Sunday, and to visit the people from house to house; the duty of the people was to attend church twice on Sunday and to hear the sermons. The congregation in those days was a quiet old-fashioned business, with a monopoly of its district, and an unquestioned hold upon its people, and was conducted without excitement or bustle.

Life, within a generation, has been electrified in every department; it has become keen, intense, inventive, an endless race, in which the most far-seeing, ingenious, adaptable outruns his neighbour and wins. One has sometimes wished that the Church of Christ had been untouched by this feverish spirit, and in the midst of a surrounding unrest had afforded a haven of peace. One, however, recognises the fact that the Church cannot live isolated and detached in the world, but that the tides of the outside world must also be felt in her life. For weal or woe—more for weal than woe—the congregation has awaked and kept pace with the times. The yearly report, with its departments of work, its various offices, its elaborate finance, rivals that of any company in commerce. Church buildings now have every kind of accommodation, from libraries and class-rooms to workshops and developing-rooms: they are lit by electricity, and the organ is played and driven by electricity; and one fearfully anticipates the day when the phonograph will be used in the pulpit, and the eloquence of famous men, living and deceased, be laid on at will. The minister is a man of affairs, issuing a yearly programme, like a business circular with its striking features and new items, supervising the most various agencies, loaded with correspondence, and carrying a diary in which he hastily books engagements like a man on the exchange. Church-work has become a science which young ministers have to learn, and the congregation is perhaps the most highly developed institution in human society. Let us review and estimate its parts. And we shall begin with—

The *Home* of the congregation, and one may lay down those principles about a church, that whatever be the style of architecture it must be (*a*) *beautiful*, because this is the House of God, and people are to meet here for His worship. The church should excel the houses of the worshippers in fineness and honesty of workmanship. Whether it be intended to hold one hundred or two thousand, whether it stand in a rich district or a poor, whether it be built of stone or brick or wood—those are matters of circumstance,—the material must be the best of its kind, and every inch of the work must be done in the sight of God, Who desireth truth and hateth iniquity. Rotten stuff, half-done work, tricky expedients, deceptive appearances, gaudy decorations, are to be condemned everywhere, but most of all where people meet in the name of Christ and pray to be created in His likeness. Better rough stone walls than gay colours hiding a lie, better bare white deal than wood stained after the likeness of mahogany, where the colour cannot hide the unworthiness of the substance. It is sufficient that a church should be nothing more at first than four strong walls and a sound roof, and that from year to year the people that have been blessed therein should give, one a painted window, another a piece of oak carving, a third a Holy Table, a fourth a font, till the church house be filled and beautified with the gifts of her children, and it is for the minister to insist on that morality which is the foundation of true beauty, and to move his people to bestow those gifts which form its crown.

(*b*) The church ought also to be *comfortable*, not in the way of softness and luxury—a place where people can lounge through divine worship, or a place fitted up with every convenience of a theatre, for it is well that people should understand that they come here on an august service, not to a social party,—but it is fitting that the church should have the best atmosphere—air cool in summer and warm in winter, and always pure. There are churches so conservative that they not only retain the former habits of thought, but the very air of the past, so that one entering after a long absence recognises the fragrance, since nothing refreshes memory like smell, and is again with his mother in the family pew, while the old minister, after preaching an hour, is giving out his third head. Were the air of one of the hermetically sealed churches bottled and analysed by some of those awful scientific inventions that are making darkness as light, it might be possible to write the history of the congregation with a likeness of the minister. The material lies in the building. Bad air is an auxiliary of Satan, and accounts for one man sleeping, for another fidgeting, for another detecting a personal attack in the sermon, for some one smelling heresy.

It was carbonic acid gas he really sniffed. And indeed the analogy is complete. Fresh air and orthodoxy go together as well as good temper and charity.

[We touch at this point the inexhaustible question of draughts, and must leave it alone, with the following observations for the comfort of the ministry :—That there never has been any church yet without a draught: that it is the only reason why certain people do not attend with regularity: that a draught of ten-horse power would not keep them from the theatre or a reception : that the officers of the church will receive fifty suggestions a year how to cure the draught, but that the genuine church draught cannot be cured by physical expedients : that, in short, it is a device of the Prince of the power of the air, as any man with Celtic blood in his veins knows.]

(*c*) And the church ought to be *convenient*, by which one means suitable for its

MACHINERY OF A CONGREGATION

purpose, a place in which every one can see and hear the preacher. There are persons who listen better with their eyes closed, and who would be content behind a Norman arch—sight distracts their mental processes,—but the majority understand with their eyes,—finding a running commentary on the preacher's words in the changing expression of his mobile face. [Nothing is trivial which concerns the success of the minister's work, and it is a grave question whether he ought not to be clean shaven, that the play of his lips, as he pleads, may further his words.]

Architecture is a noble art, and architects are doubtless of the salt of the earth, but nothing will convince me that, as a body, they ever think of the acoustic perfection of a church or of anything else, except that it be a monument to their genius. If it should happen that the people are able to hear the sermon on the day of dedication, then their gratitude is almost slavish, and it is boasted that St. Bede's is 'a good church for hearing'—they might as well have blessed the architect for giving them a roof,—while, in ten cases out of twenty, the office-bearers spend a certain proportion of their time in shifting people from pews where they cannot hear, or considering whether the minister will be able to convey his message best by a sounding-board or wires stretched across the church. It is maddening to think that in the Church of Christ a minister has to be estimated in certain places by his vocal apparatus, so that one with a voice and little else obtains a large sphere of work, and one with everything except a throat of brass is confined to a small church; but such anomalies will continue till it be legal that a church, which is useless for its purpose, be returned to the architect as a ship which, not constructed to float, would be refused by a shipowner.

With regard to auxiliary accommodation, it must vary with circumstances, but a minister, as the responsible head of the work, should insist on this minimum for a city church.

(*a*) A large hall, built on the same floor as the church, and on an ecclesiastical plan, so that when a person enters it he may have a feeling that he is in church. This is a matter of roof, windows, and reader's desk, with a general severity of treatment. All week day services, except Christmas and Good Friday, and New Year's Day, when kept, should be held here. It does not matter for effect upon the worshippers or preacher how many are present, but only that the place be full. A crowd in the hall would only be a handful in the church, and handfuls scattered about a large building can neither warm the heart for prayer nor cheer the minister for speech. The place can also be used as a gathering-place for the Sunday-school and for philanthropic meetings by reversing the chair and having a platform at the opposite end from the desk.

(*b*) A business-room fitted up with a round table, somewhat imposing chairs and chairman's seat, a safe, and case for books. Here let all the committees of the church meet, and the finance be managed. If you crush a dozen men, accustomed to other things, into a small mean room, till one has to sit on the end of a sofa and two share a chair, then, owing to the infirmity of human nature, even men of light and leading will get slipshod, and neglect not only rules of order, but also of speech.

(*c*) A ladies' room, which the women of the congregation can furnish and decorate to their hearts' content, and which shall be the centre of all their special work.

(*d*) A young people's room, almost as large as the hall, but not so ecclesiastical, where the various societies of the church will make their home, and where social meetings can be held. There ought to be bookcases for the various libraries of the church, and a collection of sacred art on the walls, as well as a case of maps. This room should be enriched as time goes on with nice pieces of furniture, till it become a drawing-room, a library, an art gallery, and a museum, besides a lecture-room on occasion.

(*e*) As many unappropriated rooms as can be got, each approaching twenty feet square, and furnished with a table, chairs, and a blackboard, for classes of any kind, fellowship meetings, and miscellaneous purposes. [One room should be allotted to the choir, and placed under the authority of the organist.]

(*f*) The minister's vestry, which should be a large, airy, well lit, and well furnished room. This is the minister's sanctum, and he gives it the last touches of habitation himself — keeping here a few favourite books, a George Herbert in the facsimile edition, the *Fioretti* of St. Francis, Rutherford's Letters, Whittier's poems, something of Christina Rossetti, that he may be in good company before he goes into his awful work : and hanging here a Perugino and an Angelico, that he may look on the Crucified and see the holy angels before he faces his fellow-men. The vestry must be regarded as the absolute property of the minister, where he can be alone and have fellowship with God before he speaks in His name, and where he can receive those who must see him alone. When a church abounds in rooms extempore meetings are not to be held in the vestry, and desultory conversations on the weather can be conducted more profitably in the lobby. Finally, if it be possible, there should be greenery and flowers round the church and in the minister's vestry according to their season, snowdrops and lilies

MACHINERY OF A CONGREGATION

and roses, for his own good and that of the people.

We come now to the *Government* of the congregation, and shall escape the most wearisome and futile of all controversies by conceding at once and without reserve the divine right of all systems—first, because they have each one been proved from the Acts of the Apostles and the Epistles of St. Paul, to say nothing of the Fathers and early centuries; and, secondly, because each of the three great systems which found themselves on Holy Scripture—the Episcopal, Congregational, and Presbyterian (the Methodists frankly admit that theirs is an invention)—has been blessed of God, and so has been sanctioned. With regard to a congregation, the first point is that there be some government, so that it be a regiment, not a mob, and the next point that the rule be in the hands of one man. Government cannot be placed in commission and twelve men divide authority. Whether the ruler be called Tzar or President, he is a necessity, and in the congregation he ought to be the minister. Who fitter than the man who has to lead, guide, represent the congregation? Who is most concerned in its success, most hurt by its failure? If not, then who is it to be? The noisiest, the wealthiest, the most obstinate? If a congregation wishes to be saved from patronage and tyranny let it support the legitimate ruler and put down any usurper. If a private member becomes lord of a congregation, then no man of self-respect will consent to be minister, and people of self-respect will refuse to take any share in the work. One of the worst calamities that can befall a congregation is such an usurpation, all the more if it has been gained by wealth, and one of the happiest events is the deposition of the usurper. Since some one must rule, the reign of the minister is the best guarantee for the freedom and harmony of the congregation, since he takes the throne in virtue of his office, and does not seize it through ambition or the giving of money.

[The minister must rule in the spirit of Jesus—with sympathy, tact, generosity, and impartiality. Ministerial government is too often discredited by coarse men, who, being raised suddenly to power, lose their heads and outrage congregations, or undisciplined natures who, by eccentricities of temper or habit, play the fool in face of the people.]

If the minister is to be responsible and actual ruler it is on that account the more necessary that he be assisted by a Council, such as is provided in the Presbyterian polity by the Court of Elders, and in the Congregational by the Court of Deacons, and which, if his system afford none, he were wise to create for himself. It should

THE CURE OF SOULS

consist of the heads of departments in the congregational work, such as the superintendents of Sunday-schools, treasurers of finance, chairman of guilds, representative of the mission church, a member of the choir committee, the officer who allocates sittings [who must be an incarnation of wisdom, patience, courtesy, and selflessness], with some venerable men of long experience, who shall sit without portfolios. This is the Minister's Cabinet, which holds all the reins in its hand, and in which every interest is represented. It is dangerous to allow bodies to rise in the Church who have no voice in the Cabinet, and over which it has doubtful control.

[In some places the Sunday-school and the Young Men's Society are simply confederated powers with the congregation, not an integral part, and the government negotiates with them.]

Colonies without share in the Imperial Government are certain, sooner or later, to start a disastrous war of independence.

When this council meets in its courtroom, with the minister presiding, it should be the brain of the congregation gathering unto itself every nerve, sensitive to the faintest feeling in the body, guiding the furthest member. Such a council at once commands the confidence and audience of the people, and the minister, sitting in council like the Pope, is in administration, so far as may be good for him and the people, infallible and absolute.

This Cabinet ought to take an unspoken oath of secrecy in order that their work may be done in freedom, and the minister ought to treat his Cabinet with unreserved confidence, not only laying before them his definite proposals, but giving them an idea of his plans, allowing his faithful councillors a share of his joys and sorrows, and taking their advice on many details of his private life. They ought to know when he goes from home, where he is, and how it fares with him, and all the changes in his life at least twenty-four hours before the public. If the Council be opposed to any of his proposals the minister had better pause, but if they approve, then he can go forward with boldness. This may be monarchy, but it is constitutional monarchy.

It goes without saying, that with so much partially sanctified human nature, there will be some insubordinate members in a congregation, who are dissatisfied with the doctrine of the pulpit or the methods of work, and feel bound to create disturbance. If they be at the bottom reasonable and pious people, then the minister will show them every consideration, explaining and conciliating as becometh a servant of Christ. If they be pharisaical or quarrelsome, then the minister had better not waste time on conferences, which will only feed such people's

MACHINERY OF A CONGREGATION

vanity, but insist with courtesy on their departure to some other church where they will feel themselves more at home. And if they should refuse, then the minister ought to consult his council and compel the mutineers to leave the ship, for a ship may weather many storms from without, but mutiny among the crew is destruction. A congregation will be stronger by the loss of a dozen people who are carping at everything, and proclaiming aloud their dissatisfaction to a district.

If, on the other hand, a person with a mutinous record should arrive, and desire to be received, he ought to be firmly refused. It is neither wise nor kindly to give welcome or have anything to do with one who has done his best to wreck a neighbouring congregation, and to embitter a brother minister's life. There is a comity of nations, and there ought to be a comity of congregations (and denominations), so that every door should be closed against the ecclesiastical anarchist. If any one inquire what is to become of him, why not have in every large city a chapel where this class could worship together, and be kept in quarantine till they show signs of penitence, when they could be absolved, and be again admitted among healthy people? And to the pastorate of this chapel of correction a minister who had wrecked two churches by bad temper and overbearing conduct might be appointed. Under such a mutual discipline both minister and people would have a good chance of being cured.

Ministers might very well copy the etiquette of the medical profession, which is distinguished by the respect its members show to one another. No minister should criticise another minister in public, nor should he allow any person to discuss his minister with him, nor should he visit the people of another minister, nor in any way, direct or indirect, try to attract them

MACHINERY OF A CONGREGATION

from his brother. Every minister should at all times stand by his brethren, and should do his brother's work for him in any time of trouble.

After a wise government, which is the brain, the welfare of the congregation depends on *fellowship*, which is the heart of the congregation. Like a college or a regiment, the congregation ought to have a just and proper *esprit de corps* which is born of high traditions, is fed by unselfish ends, is fruitful of costly services. The richest heritage of an old congregation is not her endowments, but her history, the names of saints which can be read on her faded rolls, and the record of their works. The ambition of a new congregation ought to be the attainment of a worthy model in its first plastic years. For character is transmitted in ecclesiastical as surely as in family life, so that men have the hereditary features of their congregation—a certain accent in doctrine, a certain manner in work, a certain attitude of faith.

[Certain churches, owing to high position and ancient descent, may think too mightily of themselves, and this came to my mind once when the beadle of a church in my own communion inquired of me where I was settled, and whether I was actually ordained, preparing me for a thin audience, as the Doctor was known to be from home, but cheering me before next service with the information that a fair number of people had returned—a circumstance at which he could not conceal his astonishment. If a man be not humbled after that discipline, and reduced to his low estate, then he is incorrigible. It also came home to me with much conviction that another church, also of my own communion, thought too little of itself when the office-bearers explained to me in the vestry that their minister was so learned and accomplished that he ought to be promoted, as they expected he soon would be, to a West-end church, and that the best minister for them was a plain man without too much education, 'in fact, just like yourself.' Both extremes are to be avoided.]

Congregational patriotism demands that, whatever differences of opinion the minister may have with his people, or whatever fatherly rebukes he may feel it his duty to give them, he should neither say one word against them outside, nor allow any reflection to be made upon them by a stranger. No man exposes his wife's faults, and no one dares criticise a wife to her husband; and people and minister are united in a sacred bond, sharing a common love and reputation. And the same Church feeling should keep the people true to their minister. If he has failings, or makes mistakes, they are to be covered; if he has excellencies, and does good work, that is to be told. He ought to be to his own the

THE CURE OF SOULS

ablest preacher they ever heard, and the most eloquent. People of other churches, with eminent divines, are amazed and smile at this fond imagination, for the last time the worthy man was in their pulpit he was particularly dull. To them—yes, because he was not their minister; they judged him by his poor commonplace discourse (an ambitious effort he had made for this famous pulpit! better have taken one of his simple addresses), but his people read in between the lines—his visits in sickness, his sympathy in trial, his endless kindnesses to them and theirs. They edit his sermon sitting in their pews, with footnotes that by-and-by eclipse the original till the humble building of grey stone is covered with roses and clematis, and becomes a very picture of beautiful colour. The people are fairly overcome by his lovely illustrations, his deep arguments, his moving appeals; but he did not write

MACHINERY OF A CONGREGATION

them last week, they are deeds — ten, twenty, thirty years old.

The very church has a hold on the pious mind, that grows with the years and lasts till death removes the man to the upper sanctuary. People with prosaic minds see him on Sunday morning passing a dozen fashionable suburban churches, and trudging down to a dingy place in the city, and they refer it to his old-fashioned ways and that cat-spirit which clings to a building. They do him less than justice; they have too little imagination. He has his own reasons, this unsentimental, matter-of-fact man.

[The hardest man has a tender, poetical, romantic side, and he expects it to be touched from the pulpit. He brings out his few pet flowers on Sunday morning and gives them a good exposure, in hope that their dusty leaves may be refreshed by a shower, and a bud or two open in the kindly sunshine.]

THE CURE OF SOULS

Our friend has his reasons for his city pilgrimage, and they do him credit. When he came up from the country he stumbled into that church one morning, and it seemed as if he had been expected. An elder shook him by the hand and took him to his pew; afterwards he asked him to dinner, and told him that there would be a place for him every Sunday. There is a pew in that church he could find in the dark, for there, just below that window, under the gallery twenty from the door, Christ and he met face to face. He was married in that church, and there he offered his children to God. During his great trial it was the word he heard in that church which sustained him, and down its aisles he has carried the holy vessels of the Sacrament for thirty years. He is poor who has no sacred places on earth, and this is to the man as the gate of heaven. A congregation made up of such men is like one of those ancient buildings wherein the stones have grown into a solid mass. It may be human for the suburban minister to regard this man with desire as he passes his door, for who would not wish to have so loyal a spirit? But that minister is unworthy of the name of Christ if he approves not his constancy, and thanks God his brother down town has got such a strength at his right hand.

[The opposite of this true soul is the religious nomad who changes his church every three years, who assures each minister on arrival that in his poor judgment he is the most brilliant preacher in the city, who begins by attending every service in the week, and can hardly be kept out of the mothers' meeting, who regrets that he cannot give to the funds as his means have long been consecrated in a special direction—whose wife calls towards the end of the three years to explain that she feels it her duty to go with her husband, who is receiving much benefit from a course of lectures on the Vials of the Revelation, given by the new minister of a neighbouring church. A young minister is much lifted by this enthusiastic gentleman's arrival, and somewhat cast down by his departure: an older man regards his arrival with equanimity, and suggests that he be placed in a seat which is devastated by the draught.]

We come now to the *mind* of the congregation, and it must be felt by every one that at present an enormous responsibility lies on the Church with regard to the instruction of the young (and others) in the Christian faith. Whatever may be done in State schools,—and one rejoices to know that much is done,—it is evident that the Church will have to educate her people after a thorough manner in her creed. For this purpose there ought to be an educational ladder constructed in every congregation, which will receive the young child into the infant-class of the Sunday-school at the foot, and as a man, give him the latest results of Biblical research at the top. A fully equipped congregation will have its elementary department in the Sunday-school, its secondary, or Grammar-school, in the Bible-classes for young men and women, and its University in the Bible-guild for the class who wish to pursue their studies in sacred literature.

What is needed, above all things, for the Sunday-school, is capable and trained teachers. It is worse than a mistake to hand over children to the care of some ignorant young woman (or man) who has been appointed because her mother thought she would be steadied by religious work, or because she thought it was correct to take some such task, who comes when she has no other engagement, and who does not know the bare facts of Bible history.

[One quite delightful young woman informed me, in a *viva voce* examination, that 'Herod did not get our Lord in the Massacre of the Innocents because His mother hid Him among the bulrushes.' She was a Sunday-school teacher, and just the person for whom the little mischiefs in a class would lay traps with an innocent face.]

It lies upon the minister, with the superintendent of the school, to see that no one ever obtains a class without giving some evidence of fitness, both in knowledge and teaching faculty, that the teachers attend a class where they may be drilled in the week's lesson, and that the embryo teacher be reared in the Guilds with a view to this work. When a school is staffed with well-educated teachers, then the minister can use all his influence to secure the attendance of the children of the congregation, because he can give pledges that the teaching of Scripture on

MACHINERY OF A CONGREGATION

Sunday will be on a par with the teaching of languages on the week days.

If the congregation be organised on the Guild system, then there ought to be one for young men from sixteen to thirty—no one being allowed to enter after twenty-five, or to remain after thirty (it may come to pass otherwise that the Guild consists of middle-aged men whose very appearance scares a young fellow from the door), and another for young women of a corresponding age :—age must not be looked at too curiously in this Guild, but marriage must entail retirement, since an unmarried girl and a married woman look at life from quite different standpoints. Those two Guilds may have four departments: a religious, in the Bible class which is to be thoroughly taught and examined, with occasional devotional meetings; a literary, in which good books and subjects of social interest can be discussed; a practical, which will undertake some charitable work ; and (if thought desirable) a physical, for gymnastics and excursions. There had better be a Guild for the children, called by a taking name, and holding half a dozen bright meetings every winter, in a prettily decorated room, and with liberal use of a good lantern, to interest the children in missions, temperance, and charity. When there is any considerable number of domestic servants in the church, they ought to be formed into a Guild—which will be mainly social, because they are apt to be isolated and to have little share in the church life, and because there is no class in a congregation more loyal, liberal, kindly.

The Bible Guild will crown and complete the system, and is strongly to be recommended in this day. The minister here will be president, and the members having come to years of discretion, and being, as is presumed, the most intelligent people in the congregation, will form a fellowship of students. The subscriptions will go to form a library, to which every new book with good reputation will be added, till the congregation possesses through this Guild a fairly complete collection of contemporaneous Bible literature. If the winter be divided into two terms, then, at each, one book of the Old or New Testament Scriptures is laid out for study—a careful syllabus being prepared by the committee. Papers are read by members on the authorship, history, form, ideas of the book, which will open discussion. It is remarkable what work will be put into such papers, and how grand and luminous the Bible grows under this examination.

The Society of Christian Endeavour is an alternative to the junior Guilds on the religious and practical side, but it does not embrace so wide a field, nor afford such a complete culture. It has friends and critics, but the general consensus of opinion seems to be that the movement has done much spiritual good and is likely to be an auxiliary to the Church. This is the final test of all societies in the machinery of the congregation—do they help or weaken the Church? Are they branches springing out of the trunk and gathering into their leaves the air and light of heaven—a beauty and strength? Then let them be fostered. Or are they suckers drawing away so much of the sap from the tree itself? a luxuriant, unprofitable, mutinous undergrowth — then let them be cut down and done away with, for they are in any case only human inventions, but the Church is of Christ and the home of the soul.

When we come to the *work* in the Church, it will be agreed that every large congregation should have an outlet for its energy and liberality, and I wish to urge that this, wherever possible, should be a

MACHINERY OF A CONGREGATION

church in some poor district. What is called a Mission Hall is an unfortunate form of Christian enterprise, and it is hoped will soon be obsolete. First, because it means waste of labour and worse, the hall gathering but a handful of religious paupers who come to it as to a soup-kitchen for what they hope to get, and being converted anew with every fresh distribution of alms: who almost never rise to the independence and life of a congregation, and who seem to constitute a servile body on which the philanthropy of the wealthy mother church can experiment and expend itself. If the money lavished on such unhealthy plants had been devoted to Foreign Missions or night schools, it had done ten times more good and as much less evil.

Also because such squalid places, with their half-educated agents and starved services, are an insult to working men. Why should a man not have a good church and a proper service because he earns wages and lives in a small house? If any difference be made, then the finer buildings and the lovelier worship ought to be for the east end, where there is less beauty in the homes and a harder fight for life. If the proletariat is to be won for Christ, it will not be by patronage but by brotherly sympathy and co-operation. The ideal is that a Church of the west and another of the east should go into partnership, combining their resources of means and men, and so the gaping wounds of society will be bound and healed; for Christ alone, by His humanity and Church, can be the meeting-place for all kinds and conditions of men.

All machinery, however well conceived and enthusiastically worked, will be unblessed and useless unless the Church has spiritual aims, and be touched with heavenliness, unless she be cleansed from false ideals and a worldly spirit.

MACHINERY OF A CONGREGATION

One is indeed afraid that many of our people in this material age are coming to regard the Church as a huge business concern, with its elaborate statistics, its annual balance-sheet, its endless inventions, its spirit of bustling prosperity. The world sees one congregation revive its dwindling attendance with an organ, another selling its site in a poor district and migrating to the suburbs, the amazing advertisements of sermons in the newspapers, the schemes for raising money, from bazaars to anniversaries. They do not despise the Church for these expedients; far worse—they sympathise with her. She also finds competition keen, and cannot conduct business after the old-fashioned way. She also has to cut the rates, and build bigger steamers, and puff her goods. With our elaborate financial and statistical blue-books in his hands, a layman soon creates his standard of success for a minister, and unless he be a man of very high spirituality it is certain to be tangible and material. Are all the sittings let? Are the office-bearers merchant princes? Are there Guilds of every kind and description? Is there a surplus balance at the close of the year? Then, says this shrewd, respectable man, here is a successful minister. Perhaps, but not on that evidence. Here again is a church with half its sittings unlet, with obscure names in its report, with small funds. Some want of energy here? Perhaps, and perhaps not. It may be that this man is making men, while the other has only seat-holders. The blue-books serve some purpose, and with the terror of the great permanent officials before the eyes, one dare not speak lightly of their columns; but one may protest against the success of Christ's Church being tried by figures of sittings and money.

What kind of man flourishes best in this commercial atmosphere? Not the prophet; he withers and dies in the dust

MACHINERY OF A CONGREGATION

of figures; but instead of him you will get that latest product of machinery—the organiser. No, he is not very much of a preacher or scholar, but he is a good business man and a capital manager. Let us give its due to every talent—and organising is one,—but one grows suspicious, and hesitates to have this man for his minister. Let us make him an electoral agent, or the manager of a working-class insurance company that collects by streets, or let him be sent round to clean up the house for some big heart who has so many people he can't get them into their Guild partitions. Do not hand over a number of poor souls to his preaching; it will be all from the book of Numbers. Everybody will be a secretary or something in a year, but the people will be going to the next church for their daily bread. In fact, the organiser doesn't need people; a really capable man of this type could organise a congregation on a desert island. What we want to-day is not organisers, but preachers, and every hindrance ought to be removed that a man who can preach may have an opportunity of fulfilling his high calling. One Minister laboured for three years night and day, and when His ministry was suddenly closed He had only a roomful of people. But one man was St. John and one woman was St. Mary Magdalene. A single Raphael counts more than hundreds of clever impressionist sketches. One saintly soul reared by a patient ministry will weigh down in the scales mobs of hearers.

Our illustrations have been taken from the congregation of the city, but let no man think lightly of the village church and its faithful pastor.

Where would city Christianity be without the men and women of strong, stable character that are added from the country? Who made their character? This man who is unheard of, who is too often badgered about raising money, who has the lowest stipend, who goes home feeling himself a burden on the Church. Let him lift up his head. His is lasting work, for he has wrought in imperishable material—not in silver or gold, but in the souls of men. His master knoweth : his reward remaineth. Year after year some nameless monk labours on a rough block in some cathedral column till it turns into the very likeness of Christ. He dies, and they bury him in a forgotten grave ; but every morning the light streaming through the eastern window over the head of Christ as from the eyes of the Judge touches with gold that image of the Lord wrought by His servant, and as the generations pace the aisles beneath, high above them, beautiful and unchanging, remains the unknown worker's memorial.

THE WORK OF A PASTOR

CHAPTER VII

THE WORK OF A PASTOR

WHEN the Church of Christ receives a reinforcement of common sense, and manages her affairs with as much shrewdness as a bank, one is certain that her rulers will make some salutary reforms. Incapable men will be removed without hesitation, on the sound principle that the ministry exists for the Church, and not the Church for the ministry. The man and his work will also be harmonised, so that a scholar who can find his way through documents J. E. P. and D. like a gamekeeper over a moor, will not be set to organise an East-end mission; nor will a robust evangelist, whose sermon consists of three sentences which are charged with truth but defy punctuation, be set down to minister from January to December to thinking people. Perhaps some of us may also live to see the day when four struggling congregations in the city will be amalgamated, and one large and powerful church will command and serve a district. A congregation of, say, 4000 people all told—with a church holding 2000, which would be sufficient accommodation for all likely to be present at any single service—would have various undeniable and important advantages over its four predecessors.

(*a*) The necessary sermon production would be reduced by three-fourths, and the sermon would be more telling, because the preacher would have the electrical stimulus of a mass of human life, and not have to select the largest group in a half-empty church for his practical lessons, lest, wandering hither and thither among solitariness, he might be charged with personality. It is a sin of maladministration, for which some one will have to answer, that men wear out their hearts preaching to a handful whose words might have edified thousands.

(*b*) Ministers and officers would be delivered from the harassing financial problem how to make nineteen shillings do the work of twenty, and the people from the weary drip of collection appeals, both because the income would be much larger and the expenditure would be considerably smaller. Giving is a fine grace and an excellent discipline for character, but endless and pathetic begging for money, with all sorts of expedients from bazaars to tea-meetings, is not at all within the range of grace, and aids no one's character.

(*c*) The practical work of the congregation would be carried on with vigour and an affluence both of agents and finance—the men who could give, and the men who could counsel, and the men who could work, and the men who could pray—the four who ought to lift the paralysed human mass—working in a happy partnership.

(*d*) The common life of a congregation would be free from the envies, jealousies, ambitions, and quarrels which embitter the narrower life of smaller bodies. Diotrephes is a mighty man among two hundred poor people, and threatens loudly what he will do if he does not get his own way; but when Diotrephes lands in a large congregation and finds himself of no account, he is the most agreeable and deferential of men, for there is none so mean and cowardly as the congregational bully.

(*e*) And, which is my present point, in such a congregation one minister would not be expected to fill all offices—to be a preacher, a lecturer, a teacher, an organiser, a financier, an ecclesiastic, a pastor, but there would be a staff among whom

THE WORK OF A PASTOR

the varied and complicated duties of the modern ministry could be divided.

It may be a counsel of perfection to expect that church business should be assigned to an order of ecclesiastics, who would preside at courts, draw up reports, concoct motions, carry out legislation, attend committees, and fulfil one hundred irksome duties which try the ordinary minister, and take him away from his study and his people.

[The ecclesiastic is a genus by itself, whose members may have to waste their time in the pulpit and in going from door to door, but whose mind lives and moves and has its being in the sphere of law: who discharge the most tiresome sapless work ever laid to the hands of man, with conscientious pains and accuracy, who receive no thanks from ungrateful brethren, with a boyish love for disorderliness; but who are greatly missed after they are dead, and the business which they once managed has got into a hopeless tangle. As I have seen a tree drawing its nourishment out of a bed of coal, so those patient men may find food in their marvellous phraseology, and at a time one has seen them lifted with some secret joy.]

And it may be another vain hope that the whole supervision of Biblical and theological instruction will be given in each large congregation (or group of congregations) to one of those accomplished young scholars who are now coming out from our colleges by the score, and often are broken-spirited because they can get no work to do, being inclined to read essays in the pulpit, and being afflicted with fits of painful silence in sick-rooms—who are a priceless waste product. It is, however, surely within practical affairs that this congregation of ours should have two ministers—one to be the preacher and the other the pastor. Many men combine the two gifts of the shepherd, to feed and

THE WORK OF A PASTOR

to watch, but as Nature specialises on her higher levels, it is rare that one should excel both in the pulpit and the house. One man grudges every hour outside his study, revels in books as a fish in water, can conceive no more exhilarating pleasure than reasoning out a truth to its conclusion; does not notice people on the street, and is painfully embarrassed if they notice him; hungers and thirsts for Sunday morning, when he can deliver his message. He rejoices in forty minutes' intellectual conflict with a crowd of human souls, but afterwards does not wish to see the face of man; in the reaction which follows a great effort he is company for no one, and resigns his church every Sunday evening. God made him for his work, and he does it well. His brother is cabined among books, and longs to be among people; he plans a round of visits, as one going for a pleasant tour, and yet will delay an hour because two little children, being sent with a message, insist on giving it in person; old people's faces light up at the sight of him across the street, and he must needs go over to shake hands; there is something in the grip of his hand and the sound of his voice which sends people on their way rejoicing—so simple a thing is human nature. When he enters a house there is a general stir and an adhesion of the whole household; sick people declare with solemnity that he does more for them than the doctor, and in the hour of trial the thoughts of a family turn by instinct to this man. He also is of God's designing, and wonderfully fitted for his end. Between these men there must be no comparison, for the two are the piers of the arch.

The pastoral instinct is quite unworldly, and in this utilitarian day, with its dominant precept of 'payment by results,' can hardly be understood. What the ideal pastor sees in every member of his congregation is not some one that will be of use to him because he is such a good worker, but a soul that is given him for twenty years by Christ, and whom he must prepare for everlasting life. The pastor does not delay over the appearance and circumstances of a man any more than Christ did; like his Master he pierces to the spiritual part, the real man. He is always impressed, and sometimes quite overwhelmed, by the value of the immortal soul—this soul, still plastic and unfired, for which he can do so much or so little. He trembles for it when he sees the destroyer hovering over it like a hawk poised in mid-air, and would fain have it gathered beneath Christ's wing. He tends and waters it, like a tender vine, noting every green leaf and anxiously searching for the promise of autumn. He works on it with all kinds of tools, fashioning and shaping it, as he has opportunity, after the likeness of Christ. That is a lovely legend which describes how St. John demanded of a presbyter the young man he had committed to his oversight, and when he found the young man had lapsed from the faith and become a robber, how the old apostle sought him out and fell at his feet, and would not rest till the wanderer had consented to return to the fold. It was worthy of the friend who had lain on Jesus' bosom and drank in the Master's spirit.

His people are ever in the pastor's heart, although this may not appear in his ordinary manner. He claims identity with them in their joy and sorrow and endless vicissitudes of life. No friend is blessed with any good gift of God but he is also richer. No household suffers loss but he is poorer. If one stand amid great temptation he is stronger; if one fall he is weaker. When any one shows conspicuous grace the pastor thanks God as for himself; when any one refuses His call he

THE WORK OF A PASTOR

is dismayed, counting himself less faithful. He waits eagerly to see whether one who groped in darkness has been visited by the light from on high, whether another, who seemed to have gone into a far country, has set his face towards the Father's house. One family he watches with anxiety, because he does not know how they will bear a heavy stroke of adversity, and another with fear lest rapid success in this world may wean their hearts from God. He trembles for this merchant lest he fall below the rule of Christ and do things which are against conscience; he rejoices over another who has stood fast and refuses to soil his hands. He inquires on every hand about some young man of whom he expects great things; he plans how another may be kept from temptation. One thing he cannot do: criticise his people or make distinctions among them. Others, with no shepherd heart, may miss the hidden goodness; he searches for it as for fine gold. Others may judge people for faults and sins; he takes them for his own. Others may make people's foibles the subject of their raillery; the pastor cannot because he loves. Does this interest on the part of one not related by blood or long friendship seem an impertinence? It ought to be pardoned, for it is the only one of the kind that is likely to be offered. Is it a sentiment? Assuredly, the same sublime devotion which has made Jesus the Good Shepherd of the soul. If the pastoral instinct be crushed out of existence between the upper and lower millstones of raging sensationalism and ecclesiastical worldliness, then the Christian Church will sink into a theological club or a society for social reform: if it had full play we might see a revival of religion more spiritual and lasting than any since the Reformation.

While the theologian has been often hated, and the preacher belittled, the pas-

THE WORK OF A PASTOR

tor has always been a favourite, and his beautiful duties have frequently appealed to the poetic imagination. How finely has Goldsmith touched the simplicity and saintly poverty of the village pastor, his sympathy with all kinds of suffering, and his unbounded charity; his powerful presence and spiritual succour at the last hour. But he is most happy in his description of that fond love which is in the religious sphere like the maternal instinct in nature :—

'Thus to relieve the wretched was his pride,
And ev'n his failings leaned to virtue's side;
But in his duty prompt, at every call,
He watched and wept, he prayed and felt, for all ;
And, as a bird each fond endearment tries
To tempt its new-fledged offspring to the skies,
He tried each art, reproved each dull delay,
Allured to brighter worlds, and led the way.'

Wordsworth, ever sensible to the beauty of quietness, has his pastor also :

THE CURE OF SOULS

'The shepherd of his flock, or as a king
Is styled, when most affectionately praised,
The father of his people.'

And to the grace of this conception Victor Hugo owes his noblest character, the Bishop in *Les Misérables*, who was so beloved by his people that they called him Monseigneur Bienvenu :—

'Prayer, celebration of the religious offices, alms, consoling the afflicted, the cultivation of a little piece of ground, fraternity, frugality, self-sacrifice, confidence, study, and work, filled up each day of his life.'

Nor are we to suppose that this ideal is confined to poetry, for it was at least twice realised in history,—when Richard Baxter was minister of Kidderminster, and George Herbert was rector of Bemerton. One was a Puritan, and a type of his kind: keen, restless, conscientious, ever arguing for peace, who made another place of his town ; and I copy the title-page of his book :—

THE WORK OF A PASTOR

Gildas Salvianus;

The REFORMED PASTOR.

Shewing the nature of the Pastoral work; Especially in Private Instruction and Catechizing.

With an open CONFESSION of our too open SINS.

Prepared for a day of Humiliation kept at *Worcester, Decemb.* 4. 1655.

By the Ministers of that County, who subscribed the Agreement for Catechizing and Personal Instruction, at their entrance upon that work.

By their unworthy fellow-servant
RICHARD BAXTER.
Teacher of the Church at *Kederminster*.

Luke 12. 47. Ἐκεῖνος δὲ ὁ δοῦλος ὁ γνοὺς τὸ θέλημα τοῦ κυρίου ἑαυτοῦ, καὶ μὴ ἑτοιμάσας, μηδὲ ποιήσας πρὸς τὸ θέλημα αὐτοῦ, δαρήσεται πολλάς.

The other was an Anglican, and typical of his kind: cultured, reverent, charitable, ever praying for peace, who made his parish as a colony of heaven on earth; and I copy the title-page of his book :—

A PRIEST
To the
TEMPLE,

OR
The Countrey PARSON
His
CHARACTER,
And
Rule of Holy Life.

The Authour,
Mr. G. H.

1652.

Many books on the pastoral office have been written since those two servants of Jesus entered into the higher service, and modern treatises on practical theology have their own value, meeting the changed

THE WORK OF A PASTOR

conditions of life, but none, so far as I know, have such depth of piety or such sweetness of spirit. If one prefers to read George Herbert, it is because he has more grace of letters and tenderness of soul—being orator of the University of Cambridge and a poet,—and surely nothing better has ever been written on the shepherd care of the minister than his *Parson in Circuit*, who doth not disdain to enter into the poorest cottage, 'though he even creep into it,' 'for both God is there also, and those for whom God dyed'; and who when he comes to any house first blesseth it, and then, 'as hee finds the persons of the house imployed formes his discourse.' So he passes through the parish, commending or chiding, exhorting or advising, with such tact and sincerity that it is no wonder that people blessed him as he passed, and left the plow in the furrow when George Herbert's church bell rang for prayers.

THE CURE OF SOULS

[The preacher has admiration for his peculiar reward, but the pastor has affection : if the preacher be ill there are paragraphs in the newspapers ; if the pastor, there is concern in humble homes. No man in human society gathers such a harvest of kindly feeling as the shepherd of souls, none is held in such grateful memory.]

His work, like that of a physician, may be divided into outdoor and indoor ; *visitation* and *consultation;* and one is haunted by the secret feeling that *visitation*—except in sick and special cases—is belittled by superior persons in the ministry, and regarded as a waste of time. They imagine that some of their brethren go from door to door because it is a release from the sterner work of the study, and an agreeable occupation—being a gentle form of physical exercise, and a complete rest for the mind. The visitor suggests a man delivering circulars or a lady making calls.

THE WORK OF A PASTOR

[Certain have given occasion for this caricature of the pastor, who gad about from house to house without purpose, and whose conversation is trivial gossip, who for their own sakes and other people's had better be chained to a desk daily, and receive no food till they translate one of St. Augustine's sermons. It is those weaklings who have depreciated the pastoral office and robbed it of sweet solemnity.]

With the true pastor, visitation is a spiritual labour, intense and arduous, beside which reading and study are light and easy. When he has been with ten families, and done his best by each, he comes home trembling in his very limbs and worn-out in soul. Consider what he has come through, what he has attempted, what, so far as it can be said of a frail human creature, this man has done. He has tasted joy in one home, where the husband has been restored to his wife

THE CURE OF SOULS

from the dust of death ; he has shared sorrow with another family where pet Marjorie has died; he has consulted with a mother about a son in some far country, whose letters fill the anxious heart with dread; he has heard a letter of twelve pages of good news and overflowing love which another son has sent to his mother; he has carried God's comfort to Darby and Joan reduced suddenly to poverty, and God's invitation to two young people beginning life together in great prosperity. He has to adjust himself to a new situation in each house, and to cast himself with utter abandonment into another experience of life. Before evening he has been a father, a mother, a husband, a wife, a child, a friend; he has been young, middle-aged, old, lifted up, cast down, a sinner, a saint, all sorts and conditions of life.

[This is not flexibility—the tact of a man suiting himself to circumstances,

THE WORK OF A PASTOR

but within his soul neutral and detached,—it is sympathy, the common feeling of the Body of Christ.]

It is exhausting to rejoice or to sorrow, but to taste both sensations in succession is disabling; yet this man has passed through ten moods since midday, and each with all his strength. His experiences have not all been wiped out as a child's exercise from a slate; they have become a strata in his soul.

[The coming of a beautiful idea gives the thinker a shock of delight, from which he does not recover for an hour: what must it be for one to bathe himself in the passion of humanity for five hours?]

It is not possible for the pastor to read or write after this effort of love. He is empty and helpless: he has given away himself.

The pastor of a large congregation must be very careful and methodical, and besides his ordinary pocket address-book, he attaches great importance to two books. As soon as a family comes to the church he sends them a schedule—a kind of census paper, about which there will be some simple jesting, which mollifies everything,—in which they write the names of the household and the ages of all below sixteen, telling also who are communicants and who have done church work.

[The pastoral memory grows to wonderful attainments, but it can hardly hold all the details of say three hundred families. It is not supernatural, as the people suppose, neither is his knowledge.]

The contents of this schedule are then written into a large book, finely papered and strongly bound, like a ledger; and in this book the pastor has his congregation before him at any moment. He reminds himself who ought to become communicants, or ought to take part in the church work, and where recruits can be found for the guilds and classes. Another book the

THE WORK OF A PASTOR.

pastor keeps in a drawer and shows to no one: it must be destroyed on his death. Its pages contain the spiritual history and character of his people—the results of his diagnosis—and from time to time he erases or adds to the description. Were he to show his photograph to a man, it is possible that one would not recognise himself, but that would only prove our amazing ignorance of ourselves, and the advantage of having a faithful and skilled physician.

The careful pastor will make a yearly visitation of his people, announcing his dates and localities from the pulpit, according to an ancient fashion, and he will omit no one, however rich, for he needs the pastor most; or however poor, for he will value him most. This can only be a brief visit—a mere review and interchange of greetings—but it is wonderful how much can be accomplished in fifteen minutes when the visitor is expected, when he is known and loved, when gossip is left out, and it is understood that business has to be done. One thing the pastor will not do, and that is to offer prayer in every house, because no man can pray four times an hour for an afternoon without the most miserable formality, and because prayer ought to spring out of the occasion. There are moments when conversation moves onwards till it reaches the brink of prayer. The visit then culminates and completes itself in prayer, and the petitions come from the heart. After which the pastor instantly leaves, bidding his people good-bye before the Throne of Grace, and in the very presence of the Lord.

[This regular visitation secures that no one in the congregation be overlooked; it satisfies people voracious of attention—they have had their due; it gives the people an opportunity of telling any unknown trouble, offering any suggestion, or clearing themselves of any grievance. As it progresses there is an increasing familiarity between the pew and the pulpit, till, when the last district has been overtaken, the whole congregation and the pastor are in touch.]

Sometimes the pastor receives a sudden impulse to go to a certain house, and whether it come to him in his room or on the street, he obeys it with all possible speed. On the way he will sometimes reproach himself because he may be going on a needless errand, and he will be abashed on the door-step because he has no excuse for calling. He needs none, as it appears, for he discovers in nine cases out of ten that he is needed in that house, and that his arrival is considered a providence. It is really something higher and finer — a guidance of the Chief Shepherd by the inward light of His Spirit. The pastor is convinced that if he had been more sensitive to the Divine touch, and more watchful for the Divine lead, he might have cared for the sheep with surer timeliness, and he remembers with regret many instances when Jesus called and he did not answer.

[Telepathy is not a dream nor an imposture; it is a fact within the Body of Christ, whose members suffer one with another, through the Risen Head, Who suffers with us all.]

There is one occasion when the pastor never hesitates nor delays. As soon as the message comes from the house of sickness he leaves his bed or his book, or his food or his friends, and loses no time on the way. It is possible that the summons may be needless or exaggerated; but it may not be, and he prefers to err on the safe side in the critical affairs of the soul. Even although he may be preparing his sermon, and be writing the sentence on which the whole argument pivots, he will lay down his pen between the noun and the verb. For the sermon can wait, but it may be this person cannot.

THE WORK OF A PASTOR

[Ah me! to be expected, waited for, looked for with every step and ring, and to come too late!]

On the way the pastor recalls all he knows of this person, if he be of his flock, and arranges how he will declare Christ to him; for this must be his message. He hath a scripture in readiness to give to the sick, a short, simple, tender word; and it is at such times that familiar passages revive and blossom as if it were spring with them.

[Twice does a minister learn beyond all question that the Bible contains the word of the Living God—once when he preaches the forgiveness of sins to the penitent, once when he sees a soul in the great straits of life lifted, comforted, and filled with peace and joy.]

If he ask the sick what scripture they desire, it is only a form, for there is one chapter which every man and woman want to hear in great sorrow, or when the shadow is falling. The leaf which contains the fourteenth of St. John's Gospel should be made moveable in our Bibles, in order that it might be replaced every ten years. By the time a man has got to middle age that leaf is thinning, and by old age it is only a brown film that is barely legible, and must be gently handled. Yet with every reading—say six times a week—the pastor notices that it yields some new revelation of the Divine Love and the Kingdom of Heaven. If one is sinking into unconsciousness, and you read, 'In My Father's house are many mansions,' he will come back and whisper ' mansions,' and he will wait till you finish : ' where I am ye may be also,' before he dies in peace.

[It is said that there are ministers of Christ who will not attend infectious cases, or will clutch eagerly at means of escape. If this be true—let us hope that it is a slander—the miscreant should be deposed without delay from the ministry.]

The pastor gives much of his time to *consultation*, and it is likely that he will have to give more every year. It is the custom of Protestants to denounce the confessional, and not without reason—for the claim of a priest to hear confessions and absolve is a profane interference between the soul and Christ,—but it would be wise to remember that there are times and moods and circumstances when every person desires to open his heart to some brother-man, when some persons cannot otherwise get relief. To whom are these persons to go? What they want is one who has a wide experience of life, who is versed in human nature, who is accustomed to keep secrets, who has faith in God and man, whose office invites and sanctions confidence. Who fulfils those conditions so perfectly as the minister of Christ? and is it not good that there is within reach one ordained to be a friend unto every one who is lonely and in distress of mind?

The following are the laws of consultation :

(*a*) That the pastor shall not press for any confidences, but shall receive only such as are freely offered for the relief of the person.

[Anything like prying into people's private affairs and pursuing a clue to the end is most detestable. The pastor must be thoroughly cleansed from curiosity and meddlesomeness.]

(*b*) That the pastor shall urge the person to reveal nothing more of any painful secret than may be necessary to enable him to give his advice.

[If a woman states that she has a heavy sin on her conscience, and indicates that her husband has no idea of it, then the pastor suggests that they should speak of the matter in general terms, and, if he knows the goodness of her husband, that she ought to confess the sin, whatever it may be, to him. Afterwards the pastor advises her how to meet and overcome this sin if it should arise again, and so this human soul has not been put to shame, but has gained help without losing self-respect.]

(*c*) That the pastor, although he has taken no oath of secrecy, regards every confidence as absolutely sacred, and will on no account, except at the command of the law, reveal what has been told him in consultation.

[Whosoever holds the pastoral office must learn to keep secrets, and must be on his guard against careless speech. What he has to fear is not dishonour through wilful breach of trust, but mere leakiness. The pastor does not consider his own wife a privileged person in this matter, for though she might be the most prudent and reticent of women, yet it would embarrass his people to know that their secrets were shared with her. The high honour of doctors, who carry in their breasts so many social tragedies, is an example to be followed by the clerical profession.]

(*d*) That the pastor will give such practical advice as he can, especially urging restitution, reformation, watchfulness, as the case may require.

[As he grows older he will know many precedents, and be furnished with many aids for emergencies.]

(*e*) That the pastor will not fail, so far as he may be able, to lead every person who consults him to accept Christ as his Saviour and Friend, so that all the straits of life, its sins, sorrows, disasters, may compel the soul to the faith of Christ.

What costs the pastor much more anxiety is the diagnosis and treatment of spiritual diseases, and here he has to be most careful. He distinguishes between an honest sceptic, whose face is toward the light, and who longs to believe, from one whose back is wilfully turned on Christ, and who is filled with intellectual pride: a merchant whose satisfaction comes from far-seeing and masterly strokes in business, and whose attitude is that of a soldier with his tactics, and another whose whole interest is accumulating wealth, and whose heart is world-eaten: a young man of rich, strong nature who is fighting the flesh with all his might, and another who is feeding his imagination with evil books, and preparing for the sin into which he falls: one woman full of genuine emotion, which has to be guided in the service of Christ, and another whose studied sentiment, like the soft beauty of a peach, covers a heart of stone: that woman whose tongue is a danger through her endless good-natured garrulity, this one who does cruel injury by clever detraction and calculated slander. If any one is wounded in his feelings, he will examine whether this arises from tenderness of heart or from mortified pride ; and if any one bear the criticism of life unmoved it is a question for him whether this be self-control or self-conceit. Where the spiritual health of a family is evidently suffering, he finds out whether the husband is deteriorating through contact with his wife, or he be her despiritualising influence. But he is never meddlesome, censorious, unsympathetic. With every year he sees more of the temptations of life and the goodness of human nature. For the innocent gaiety and lighter follies of youth he has a vast toleration, for the sudden disasters of manhood an unfailing charity, for the unredeemed tragedies of age a great sorrow. It is a hard fight for every one, and it is not his to judge or condemn ; his it is to understand, to help, to comfort—for these people are his children, his pupils, his patients; they are the sheep Christ has given him, for whom Christ died.

One's heart goes back from this eager, restless, ambitious age to the former days, and recalls with fond recollection the pastor of his youth, who had lived all his ministry in one place, and was buried where he was ordained—who had baptized a child, and admitted her to the sacrament, and married her and baptized her children —who knew all the ins and outs of his people's character, and carried family history for generations in his head—who was ever thinking of his people, watching over them, visiting their homes, till his familiar figure on the street linked together the past and the present, and heaven and earth, and opened a treasure-house of sacred memories. He prayed with a lad before he went away—his mother could almost repeat the words; he was constantly inquiring about his welfare, so binding him to his faith and home by silken ties;

THE CURE OF SOULS

he was in the house on the day of his return, to see how it had fared with him in the outer world. People turned to him as by an instinct in their joys and sorrows; men consulted him in the crises of life, and, as they lay a-dying, committed their wives and children to his care. He was a head to every widow, and a father to the orphans, and the friend of all lowly, discouraged, unsuccessful souls. Ten miles away people did not know his name, but his own congregation regarded no other, and in the Lord's presence it was well known, it was often mentioned; when he laid down his trust, and arrived on the other side, many whom he had fed and guided, and restored and comforted, till he saw them through the gates, were waiting to receive their shepherd-minister, and as they stood around him before the Lord, he, of all men, could say without shame, 'Behold, Lord, Thine under-shepherd, and the flock Thou didst give me.'

THE PUBLIC WORSHIP OF GOD

CHAPTER VIII

THE PUBLIC WORSHIP OF GOD

It is vanity for Christians to shut their eyes to the fact that attendance at public worship is decreasing, and that this is not a hopeful omen for religion. Ingenious advocates may make the best of this tendency, and may bring forward various saving pleas—that public worship is rather an example than a commandment of Holy Scripture; that God is not confined to any house made with hands, and can be found as surely in the green fields, or in a good book, as in an ecclesiastical building; that some of the worst people are conspicuous by their presence, and some of the best by their absence; and that the dreariness of service, as well as the stupidity of many sermons, is fitted to dull rather than quicken the religious spirit. When this clever person is in a lighter mood, he allows himself to make play with the conventionalities and eccentricities of public worship, but when he rises to his height, he speaks with tears in his eyes of a certain sunset which you are assured has done more for his soul than all the sermons he ever heard.

One may frankly grant the force of any one of those arguments, and at the same time remind our friend, what he knows very well, and every other person, that he has not gone to the root of the matter. Granted that some people go to church to whom worship must be a vain show, and that others remain at home to whom it is a spiritual reality, it were quite absurd to divide people into public worshippers who are professional hypocrites, and private worshippers who are unattached saints. As a bare matter of fact, believing people do, as a rule, go to church, and unbelieving people, as a rule, do not: and in order to show that one is not using faith in a dogmatic but a vigorous sense, it may be sufficient to point out that on the Church —her teaching, her influence, her example —the whole system of charity and philanthropy depends in the Western world.

The contrast is not between those who worship in churches and those who worship at home, but between those whose faith in the Risen Christ is so real and strong that it draws men together on the first day of the week to celebrate His resurrection, by which He has become the Living Way unto the Father, and those to whom this chief event in human history is a fond imagination, and whose idea of God is so vague and impersonal, that they can find Him in the running of a stream as surely as in the face of Christ.

Various reasons of secondary importance may of course be given for the decay of this great function of faith, and they ought to receive serious consideration at the hands of the rulers of Christ's Church. Perhaps the austere conception of God as Sovereign and Judge, which held the souls of our fathers in an irresistible grip, has been replaced by a too easy and familiar attitude of thought. Where there is no awe there will be little worship. With this weakening of the Divine fear has come, as a natural consequence, a relaxation of parental authority, and congregations are thinner to-day because, while in the past a father took order that all his children of convenient age should be with him in the family pew, children now attend church, or not, as they please,—the likes or dislikes of ten-year-olds about preachers and sermons being seriously considered.

[The father is God's viceroy, but if God has ceased to have authority, a father can hardly be expected to rule.]

It is also more than likely that the multiplication of religious work and of peculiar services, with strange ways and sensational attractions, compete with public worship ; and it is a grave question whether bizarre services, each one of which is vaunted in turn as a new attraction to religion, are not a depreciation of the Church of Christ. When each one of those causes has been credited with its own drain, it remains that worship rises or falls as men believe or disbelieve in the unseen, and that the Church must give her strength to make her worship a magnificent and convincing testimony that Jesus did rise from the dead the third day according to the Scriptures.

Public worship is a demonstration of the first order, and serves the most practical ends. If one believes in a historic event, such as the achievement of national independence, or desires to see a great measure carried, such as the freedom of the slave, he joins with others of a like mind; they organise a procession, with music and banners; they hold a mass meeting, with fiery speeches and stirring resolutions. 'What folly!' says some high and mighty person; 'what good is there in this marching and oratory?' He is not only cynical, he is superficial. Has he never heard the tramp of many feet, and wanted to keep step? has he never been in a big flood of human life and been carried away? Deny a people the right of public meeting, and you have quenched the fires of enthusiasm and almost killed the hope of progress. Isolation and loneliness are the nursery of depression and pessimism; with the multitude are joy and strength. Faith is an inherent faculty of the soul, and is not independent of the laws which regulate human nature. For a week a man has been living in an atmosphere of sense, seeing and touching till the unseen fades into a dream. Is there

THE PUBLIC WORSHIP OF GOD

a world behind this painted curtain, or does it cover the wall of our tomb? Are the last chapters of the Gospels only a pious invention, the afterglow of a sun that has sunk in night? Is the Christian creed, with its hope of everlasting life, a worn-out superstition? Busy with many affairs, and separated from Christian fellowship, the man finds his faith fading and shrivelling. The light pricks his eyelids, and he awakes on the first day of the week: he rises with gracious remembrances in his mind, and sees a little company hurrying to some church where there is an early tryst between them and their Lord, Who this day burst the tomb and rose a great while before dawn. To-day there is no traffic on the streets, and weary men are resting from their labours. By-and-bye a bell breaks the stillness, and is answered from a distant tower; bells from every quarter join in, till the air vibrates and quivers with gladness. Our dispirited friend cannot resist the invitation, and he finds the street alive with people marching along with firm, composed tread. Within the church he is one of fifteen hundred, all gathered in the name of Christ, all calling Him Lord. The minister gives out the hundredth Psalm, and from nave and transepts and galleries pours forth one volume of praise:

> 'All people that on earth do dwell,
> Sing to the Lord with cheerful voice.'

Amid the mass of living, pulsating faith this solitary man's fears and doubts vanish, and he comes out into the sunshine, established afresh in the faith of the Risen Lord, his life caught up into the life which is hid with Christ in God. It is a great reinforcement to multiply a single faith by fifteen hundred.

> 'He is not risen, no—
> He lies and moulders low;
> Christ is not risen,'

so the world says, in many ways, for six days, and then the Church gathers together her children, and declares with fuller meaning than Clough intended :

> 'In the great gospel and true creed
> He is yet risen indeed,
> Christ is yet risen.'

If public worship is to feed faith in her straits, and fill the soul with heavenliness, then it must be a beautiful function, to which the minister in our day ought to give loving study and attention.

[There are churches which depreciate the service, and churches which depreciate the sermon, and both err, because sermon and service are not rivals but auxiliaries, the service spiritualising and softening the heart for the message of God, and the Evangel being the answer to the praise and prayer.]

One cannot treat of the conduct of service without touching on the comparative advantages of a liturgy and free prayer.

[It is too late to discuss the lawfulness of a prayer-book, for that indeed was settled when Jesus was pleased to give the disciples the Lord's Prayer: as the dear old Scotch lady said—yielding unwillingly to its introduction by her minister,—'I have no particular objection to that,' although she evidently felt it a dangerous precedent. The dislike to a prayer-book in a certain quarter is not theological: it is historical. If a man declines to use a liturgy, and you crop his ears and slit his nose to encourage him, human nature is so constituted that he is apt to grow more obstinate, and to conceive a quite unreasonable prejudice against the book.]

This is the case for a liturgy such as the Prayer-book of the Anglican Church:—

(*a*) That a liturgy, whose materials have been drawn from the classical ages of devotional literature, has a certain stateliness of thought and charm of style which satisfy the ear and cling to the memory.

(*b*) That a liturgy, being instinct with the spirit of undivided Christendom, will lift its children out of sectarian and provincial ideas of religion and bring them into the communion of the Church Catholic.

(*c*) That a liturgy being framed for the use of the Body of Christ, not to express any individual mood or experience, will embody the ordinary wants of all kinds and conditions of men.

(*d*) That a liturgy makes the worshippers independent of the officiating clergyman, so that his faults do not hinder their devotions.

(*e*) That a liturgy, affording a common and uniform means of worship, serves to bind together all the members of a church, both old and young, into one fellowship and loyalty.

(*f*) That a liturgy is especially suitable

for old people, because of its unchanging form of words; for people wearied by the week's toil, because their minds are not strained following a prayer through an unknown country; for young people, because their interest is sustained, and they have some part in the worship.

(*g*) That a liturgy can be taught to children from early years in the church, and unto their last days they will love and respond to the dear familiar words.

For the custom of free prayer—where the Church does not supply her children with the means of common worship, but each minister makes his prayers for the occasion—this case may be put:—

(*a*) That it encourages the grace of prayer bestowed upon the Church by the coming of the Holy Ghost, Who intercedeth within us, as Christ intercedeth for us, in the heavenly places.

(*b*) That free prayer gives to the service a certain life and freshness which are impossible when the same form is used every day from January to December, from year to year, from century to century.

(*c*) That with free prayer it is possible to render thanks for great mercies which may have been received of God, to seek His help in sore straits that have come upon us, with particular and comforting reference.

(*d*) That free prayer allows, in the experience of many, a tenderness of heart and a nearness to God that are not possible under any form.

It is well to recognise that the diversity of human nature should have full play in the Church, and as there will always be different systems of doctrine, so there ought to be different methods of worship. Some minds are churchly, reserved, delicate in their religion; they require a liturgy, since the idea of their devotions being led by one who could ask whatsoever he pleased for the congregation would only disgust and alienate them. Other minds are individualistic, frank, robust; they will not be content with a book, but rejoice in the thought of perfect freedom in prayer, and are willing on occasion to encourage their leader with sympathetic exclamations. It is possible, of course, that there may be a *rapprochement* between the two methods, as Churches with liturgies shorten or adapt them, and Churches without liturgies insist on some order of service, and even prepare forms of prayer for the use of their ministry. The ultimate issue for the Church in general might be a combination of liturgical and extemporaneous prayer.

One factor in the situation must receive due weight, and that is the growth in culture within the half-century and its legitimate influence on worship. People have more sensitive ears and a keener appreciation of perfection: they detect slipshod phrases, and are offended by any vulgarity of thought : they will not endure that a coarse man should harangue the Almighty at the pitch of his voice, or a weak man go maundering into His presence in their name. They are careful as to the furnishing of their homes, as to their clothing, as to their friends, as to their books. They shrink from what is loud and glaring ; they love what is dainty and lovely ; they appreciate fine shades, graceful manners, finished style. When these people come into the House of God, and address themselves to the highest act of life, they cannot lay aside this habit of mind, and do not see any reason why they should. They cherish the belief that the service of the Church ought to represent the very ideal of thought and feeling and language, that from beginning to end there must not be one jarring note in the spirit, or one infelicitous expression in the form. It is open to say that such people are critical, and that bad grammar has often expressed a full heart. But they insist that they are simply reverent, and that bad grammar does not express their heart. Private worship may be on the level of each family, but public worship must be on the highest. They also point out that the prayers of the Bible, whether in the Psalms or Epistles, are cast into very stately language, and yet it is not to be expected that any one will say that the Psalmists or St. Paul lacked in fervency. They will be perfectly satisfied if the prayers of the Church, however composed, should be after the grand style of Holy Scripture; but they refuse, when they bow their souls before God, to have for their mouthpiece a minister whose ideas and words outrage their feeling of good taste and reverence. Let him pray after this fashion when he is alone, for then he is speaking for himself; let him, if better cannot be got, preach, for then he is speaking to men, but it is not fitting nor just that he should conduct public prayer. This is an unanswerable contention, and cannot be despised.

We are all aware, of course, that in every Church there is a number of ministers to whom has been very richly given the spirit of grace and supplication, and who lead the devotions of God's people with tenderness and beauty. Worship under their charge combines the perfect form of a liturgy with the loveliness and spontaneity of spoken prayer. If the Church could furnish every one of her congregations with such a minister, then little could be said for a prayer-book; but every one knows that such men are the elect. We remember with unfeigned gratitude those anointed priests who went in our name into the Holiest of all, and who presented unto God what was in our hearts with the fragrance of their piety upon every word; but we also remember how others, to whom God had not been pleased to give such grace, misrepresented a thousand people woefully, asking things we did not desire, omitting to ask many things we did desire, and asking everything in terms we had never dreamt of using to a local dignitary. Without question we have suffered loss, and it is no compensation to assure us that the minister was a good man, or that he proved himself a forcible preacher.

When the Church of Christ of any branch assembles a congregation of her people together for divine service, and commits its conduct to the absolute discretion of one man, she undertakes an enormous responsibility. Has she not entered into a covenant with those present that this man will be their mouthpiece, and that all the ordinary and general wants of a body of human beings will so far as possible be presented before the Throne of Grace? Suppose, through the carelessness, or forgetfulness, or ignorance, or idiosyncrasy of this minister, no prayer is offered for the country and its rulers, or for the sick and dying, or for the sorrowful, or for those in danger on the sea, or for distant friends, or for little children, or for those who have lost the kindly light of reason, or for prodigals, or for those who have secret trials;—suppose there be no thanksgiving for the gifts of Providence, for deliverance from disease, for succour to the soul, for increase of light, for the coming of Christ, for the indwelling of the Holy Ghost, for the victory of the departed, for the life everlasting;—will there not be hundreds who entered the church laden with the weight of care or gratitude, and who hoped to the end, but hoped in vain, for relief? Can any service where such petitions and thanksgivings are absent be called public worship?

Where the Church provides no liturgy,

the minister must give great care to the service of prayer, and there are certain faults against which he will do well to guard. One is *Preaching* in prayer. When the minister expounds a doctrine of the truth, though this be the atoning sacrifice of our Lord; when he repeats a varied and quite unrelated cento of texts to which the speeches of Hebrew prophets on public affairs, and some of the most foolish utterances of Job's friends, largely contribute; when he exhorts his people to repentance and faith, or to some practical duty of the Christian life; or when he confounds sceptics, and corrects the errors of the day, treating with much unction those points wherein he conscientiously differs from his brethren, he has gravely mistaken and misused his opportunity.

Another is *Egotism*—when the minister does not seem able to distinguish between his study and the church, or his own private experiences and the needs of the

THE PUBLIC WORSHIP OF GOD

congregation, but gives himself to the fervent and often affecting exposition of his own doubts and fears, and hopes and anxieties, finally disappearing out of reach and understanding in a cloud of mystical language.

['Do you suppose,' said an excellent man of the subjective school, 'that I am to be interrupted to pray for sailors when I am wrestling before the Mercy-seat?' His wrestling, however, was not petitions for the people, but an explanation of the state of his own soul, and the sailor's mother was not greatly comforted by his lamentations.]

A third fault is *Slovenliness*—when a minister embarks on the great affairs of prayer without a chart or compass, knowing not whither he may be carried, but hoping to arrive somewhere; when the congregation are certain that he does not know what he will say next sentence; when he toils with a refractory sentence for a while, and finally lets it go in despair—hiding his defeat by a hasty outburst of artificial fervour, and when he drops into painful colloquialisms which would not be tolerated in the humblest public address.

[This style of prayer is excused on the ground of godly familiarity—two words which do not go well together: it ought to be condemned on the ground of ungodly impudence.]

Perhaps the worst offence is *Profanity* —when that man whose soul ought to be most full of awe, sprinkles his prayer with the name of the Deity, which is accompanied by no adjectives of adoration, and is shouted aloud; or when a sinful man composes a speech stiff with embroidery of rhetoric and figures, and makes an empty pretence of addressing it to God, while he is evidently calculating its effect on his audience of fellow-sinners; or when some thin-blooded and venomous creature abuses his sacred position and utilises the privilege of prayer to attack some person of his congregation who has resisted his will or done him some slight injury.

If any one desires to perfect the form of his prayers, then he can do no better than read from time to time the liturgies of the Early Church, and the choice books of Christian devotion — a collection of which should lie handy to the minister's hand. There are moments when one lays down the pen in weariness or perplexity of thought, then let him take a draught from one of those ancient wells, and he will not only be immediately refreshed, but it will come to pass that he will catch the very style of the saints, not through laborious imitation, but as one who keeps high company acquires the manners of his host.

If one desires to complete the substance of his prayers, it is wise to form a litany for himself with much care and pains—collecting all the ordinary petitions which occur to him, or are suggested by his experience as a minister, and inquiring from time to time whether any one of his people has one he knew not of, and then casting them all into order and simple tender words of devotional speech, adding a confession of sin and a general thanksgiving. This he will call the Prayer of Intercession, and use daily without fail or change, save for a few special collects which can be inserted in their season, say for colleges and schools at their re-opening, or for an election, or for a harvest, for the meeting of a Church court, and such like. [Conservative people will not object to the use of this form, but will come to love it—complaining if a word be changed.]

Worship culminates in the administration of the Sacraments, which our Lord gave us as the quickeners of the Christian life, and which are the seals of our faith. One is to be administered with great solemnity, with a Holy Table set apart for this end, and guarded from every other use, with pure white linen on the pews, in token that the people are gathered at Christ's board, with grave sweet melody, with minute observance by the minister of every symbolical word and action of the Lord, with thanksgiving for the Church triumphant, with supplication for the Church militant, in the hush of the church while the elements are carried down the aisles, and the silent, awestruck people pledge themselves anew to their Lord in the mystery of His Body and Blood.

The other Sacrament had better have a service unto itself, after the benediction in the morning, for which parents and children could remain, and the minister should make a little address on the mystery of love and the beauty of holiness, and the excellence of the religious life, and on Jesus as the Good Shepherd of the soul and the Friend of little children; and the people should stand at the act of Baptism, and the choir should chant 'Amen' when the child is baptized into the threefold Name; and there should be a short form of prayer, which the minister can compose for himself, with a thanksgiving for the gift of the child and the recovery of the mother, and a committing of the little one into Jesus' care, and a prayer for grace to be given to the father and mother for the child's upbringing, and a petition that the child heart should be kept in all present till they come to our Father's House. And there should be bright music and joyful hymns.

[Unto this service will frequently remain old men and women that have never been married, who will often speak to the mother and lift up her heart by praising the child—lonely souls in whom the love of God dwelleth richly.]

Public worship ought to be comforting, joyful, enthusiastic, beautiful, the flower of all the week, but its chief note should be reverence and godly fear. Praise and prayer, the reading of Holy Scripture, and the preaching of the Evangel, should conspire to lift the congregation above the present world and the sensible atmosphere in which they have been living, and bring them face to face with the Eternal. It was this tender and gracious fear which made the glory of Puritan faith and gave visible force to Puritan character. Nothing is more urgently needed in this day, which knows how to doubt and jest, but is forgetting how to revere and adore, when the great function of worship has become pleasing and amusing, a performance and a comedy. What we may well pray for is a baptism into our fathers' penitent, austere, enduring Christian faith, who summoned themselves hourly to the judgment-seat of Christ, and therefore considered it a small thing to be judged of man's judgment, who never met in the Great Name, whether in stately cathedral or bare hillside, but they came to the spirits of just men made perfect, and to Jesus, the Mediator of the new covenant, and to God, the Judge of all.

THE MINISTER'S CARE OF HIMSELF

CHAPTER IX

THE MINISTER'S CARE OF HIMSELF

As it is the will of God that the Church should be fed and guarded by a human ministry, there is no man on the face of the earth who has such responsibility, and who ought to take such care of himself, as the minister of Christ. And first he must see to his *health*, for the spiritual prosperity of a congregation depends very largely on the minister being not only sound in doctrine but also sound in body. It is not merely that a valetudinarian is a source of endless anxiety to kind-hearted people who have enough concern in their own homes without the burden of the minister's weakness, and that the work is certain to be crippled with a leader that is afraid of breaking down, but, what is much more unfortunate and injurious, the invalidism of his body will certainly creep into his teaching, for, as a rule, one can only get robust sermons from a robust man.

One ought indeed to be thankful that Christ chose as His first apostles men not only of conspicuous spiritual genius, but also of a hardy, natural, wholesome habit of life—fishermen, and such like,—and that of the four Gospels that must remain for ever the authoritative documents of our faith, three proceeded, directly or indirectly, from those weatherbeaten Galileans, and the fourth from a physician. Whatever may be said of later Christian literature, there is nothing sickly, unreal, mawkish, or gloomy in the Gospels. They are sober, sensible, downright, manly books, such as able-bodied men would write and real men like to read. The body is a factor in thinking, as well as in pulling ropes and forging iron. Suppose two men be both saints, you need not expect equally good stuff from each in the way of thought if one be sound in body and the other unsound. As a rule, any one who has inherited an inferior constitution, or whose nervous system is overwrought, or whose body is deformed, or who is a chronic dyspeptic, or who is in any way below the working average of strength, will be peevish in temper, inclined to useless argument, fiercely intolerant of other people's views, a slave to crotchets, and pessimistic in the extreme. It is his misfortune, and allowance ought to be made for it. He may live above it, but the chances are he will not. One ought to extend to him every consideration, as to a crippled man, but it is wise to make some discount from his opinions. Unless he be singularly assisted by the grace of God, as certain like Pascal and Baxter evidently were, they will be less than true: he is sub-normal, and his views are apt to be sub-normal too—deficient in balance, sobriety, charity. When a minister is untouched in wind, sturdy in limb, clean in blood, you have a certain guarantee of bright, honest, manly thinking. He is not likely to be falsetto, hysterical, garrulous, simply because he is sound in body as well as in mind.

[It is, however, possible to be exasperatingly healthy, and one can understand a much tried woman being driven away from a minister whose radiant unlined face showed that he had never known pain, and who had married a rich wife, and taking refuge in a church whose minister had a liver and preached rampant Calvinism. 'Was yon a man'—so she put it—'for a widow with seven children to sit under?' Invalid ministers have a certain use and do gather sympathetic congregations — becoming a kind of infirmary chaplains. But their ecclesiastical and theological views must be taken with great caution.]

It is not extravagance to say that the physical health of theologians has affected the religious character of nations. No one can estimate how much Germany has gained from Luther's genial and robust nature, or Scotland lost through Calvin being a chronic invalid and Knox being a broken man. During long centuries it was the custom of Christendom for a baron to send his able-bodied sons to the field and any deformed or sickly lad to the Church. Was it wonderful that theology and religion got out of touch with life, and became fantastic and unreasonable? Human life has now more doors for the infirm, and the Christian Church has ceased to be a home for incurables, but it is not as a rule the strong, stirring, full-blooded boys of a family who enter the ministry, but the lad who is half-alive, who plays no games,

THE CURE OF SOULS

who is painfully composed. This is a public misfortune, since, if any other man be out of sorts, his wife suffers, but if a minister be below par a thousand people have a less successful life for a week. His business is to put heart in them for six days' work and trial, but for that enterprise a man's pulse must beat high and his own heart be buoyant. If his digestion be bad, then he goes into the pulpit and hits viciously at some heresy or mourns the decay of morals. The people, who have been expecting a glimpse of heaven, go home in despair. The saints lament the degeneracy of the times, and the young people resolve that they will have nothing to do with religion. But the times are really the best we have ever seen, and religion is the strength of the human soul. The trouble is in this case neither in the Bible nor the world, but in the pulpit, which that day was filled by a hypochondriac or a melan-

THE MINISTER'S CARE OF HIMSELF

choliac. Every church should have a physical examination at the entrance to the theological college and only admit those men who would have passed as first-class lives with an insurance company. And the working minister should have his own rules of health—to have his study re-charged with oxygen every hour, to sleep with his bedroom window open, to walk four miles a day, to play an outdoor game once a week, to have six weeks' holiday a year and once in seven years three months—all that his thought and teaching may be oxygenated and the fresh air of Christianity fill the souls of his people.

He must also guard and husband his *time* with unrelenting jealous resolution; for if he fail to do so in this day, his work will dwindle down into a mere round of religious and secular trifles.

Imagine the contrast between the student's ideal of the ministry and its actual practice. It may not be given to every man to hear that sudden and irresistible voice that came to St. Francis when he left the supper-table, and, standing below the blue of the Umbrian sky, knew he was called of God to abandon all for Christ's dear sake; but within the heart of every true man the intention of the holy ministry is associated with romantic dreams and hopes. He does not expect a material reward, and he is prepared for hard work. He is willing to brave opposition and reproach to fulfil God's will; every sacrifice will have its compensation in those moments of reverent study when his heart suddenly burns within him and he knows Christ's presence is in the room, in hours when he can see the soul of his hearers leap into their faces in response to the Evangel, in days spent in carrying the Lord's consolation to the afflicted. Pardon his illusions; he is still young and ingenuous;

the student sees himself the prophet of God's truth, the shepherd of human souls. Lay down this poem, and take his diary, ten years later, when he is the minister of a city charge, and, so far as opportunity goes, has come to the height of his ministry.

Monday, the minister, exhausted by Sunday's work, faces a pile of letters that has accumulated in the end of the week, with disgust and rebellion. They are on all kinds of subjects, from a schedule issued by some committee voracious of statistics to a note of charming irrelevancy from a lady about a cook that had once been in his congregation. Two hours of clerk's work for at least five days a week was not a part of his original programme, and it is that item which whitens men's hair. His note-book shows that an Ecclesiastical Court meets in the afternoon, and after a battle with his lower self, which leans to golf, he attends, in all the glow of moral victory, to find its members engaged in persuading some poor congregation to give an extra five pounds to some fund, and afterwards throwing themselves into the discussion of a point of order with unaffected delight. In the evening he is due at a meeting which has now risen from a soiree to a conversazione, and is just bordering on a reception, where, finding six other neighbours, he contents himself with explaining the interesting circumstances in which he first met their esteemed pastor at a hydropathic.

Tuesday morning he spends at the local School Board, trying to discover under the rules how much an ex-pupil-teacher ought to get as an assistant mistress, and whether a charge of 2s. 6d. expended by the caretaker on his coal-cellar can be charged against the rates. He does visit one or two sick that day, but is hampered by an afternoon tea, where he meets seven ladies, whose husbands, being business men, were not expected to come. In the evening he presides at the Young Men's Society, which can only be kept up by his watchful presence, and hears a paper on Julius Cæsar, on which he offers remarks hurriedly gathered from an encyclopædia, but suggestive of omniscience.

Wednesday morning is occupied in drawing up a report on the debt of a church for a board, and at three o'clock he moves a resolution at the annual meeting of the Society for the Reformation of Tramway Boys. He counts himself fortunate in saving two hours for the preparation of his address for the mid-week service.

Thursday opens well, and the minister begins to work for Sunday, when a visitor comes, and then a crowd—a young lady who is anxious to be a nurse; a young man (who was once at the young men's sermon) to get a testimonial for a situation; a member of the church with no business, who wished to introduce a country friend; the travelling secretary of some third-rate society, whose time is paid; an elderly person who got good from one of the minister's sermons in a strange church, and borrows five shillings. In the evening he takes the chair at the deacons' meeting, where the main features are the church officer's salary, and a draught which is the alleged reason of the irregular attendance of two families.

On *Friday* that good angel, the minister's wife, comes to the rescue, and gives strict orders that no one shall be admitted. The outside world struggles on without apparent disaster, and the minister has the luxury of four hours' consecutive thought. If he had many forenoons like this he might become a preacher. He is, indeed, so intoxicated with study that he proposes to have a long evening with his books, when he recollects an engagement to meet the workers at Bethesda—a mission

THE MINISTER'S CARE OF HIMSELF

hall on unsectarian principles, which a member of his own church supports at the cost of £200 a year, and where he preaches to a select audience of seventy children and thirty adult pensioners. The minister wishes for the moment that he had refused to have anything to do with this mistaken form of Christian enterprise, and persuaded the good man to have aided a poor church with his liberality; but the minister has not more moral courage than other people, and he was afraid of being called unevangelical instead of sensible. But *Saturday!* This will make up for all. Alas! his wife goes off guard, and a picturesque foreigner from the East takes possession of the study. The minister, courteous as one ought to be to distant strangers, lays himself out to extricate the visitor's meaning, and after an hour's patient exploration discovers that his caller comes from an unknown place, that he represents himself, that he wishes to build something, that he is determined to preach in the minister's church tomorrow for a collection. When the man from Mesopotamia has been induced to depart, it is in vain to take up the sermon till evening. So far as I know, these details are not exaggerated, and they are given at length for a serious purpose. It is not to suggest that Christ's minister should hold himself aloof from the great charities or social causes which are the glory of national life, or be indifferent to the extension of God's kingdom or the work of foreign churches. No man is wearied or harassed by an enterprise of the first order. He is done to death by petty details, by useless talk, by religious faddists, by unnecessary correspondence. Why should a minister be concussed into the service of all kinds of trumpery societies? Has not the full time come when he ought to be released from the burden of financial affairs, whether building a church or assisting a dozen business men to administer a few hundred pounds? Is it necessary that the minister should be present at every church committee? Is there to be no finality in church organisation? Is the minister to be more and more dragged away from his chief work into every new scheme of social reformation? The ministry will have to take a stand and put it to their people whether they desire preachers or general agents, for if a man is to be in any degree a prophet he must not be driven along the dusty highways of life from Monday till Saturday, but must be allowed days of absolute quiet wherein the thoughts of God may arise and take shape in his soul.

It is absolutely necessary that the minister manage his affairs with discretion, for in his case it will not be possible to separate his private from his public life. The question of voluntary celibacy is one he ought to face before his ordination and settle his duty by his calling of God. An unmarried man can give himself without reserve to the work of the Evangel amid the dangers of heathen lands or the squalor of our great cities: he is free from worldly cares and social entanglements: he requires little from the Church and he is at her absolute disposal. If a man decide that it is God's will he should marry, then of all men he ought to be most careful in the choice of his wife, for she may be either a help or a hindrance not merely to his comfort but to his work. [One does not mean that a minister had better marry a woman who can preach or conduct meetings, in order that he may divide his duties with her, any more than one would advise a doctor to marry a nurse to assist him with his cases. Every self-respecting man does his own work, and refuses to throw any of its burden on his wife. Those stories of ministers who read their sermons to their wives before they are preached—so depriving the poor woman of any edification on Sunday or doubling her trial—and afflict her with all the little worries of his work, are wicked inventions. A minister is quite as manly as a doctor or lawyer, and knows that his wife has enough to do in her own department.] It is not the speaker who really fulfils the wife's part, nor the quiet woman who fails by the minister's side. She is a good wife who manages his house with skill and economy, so that he has to give no thought to domestic affairs, who brings up her children in the Divine Love, whose father has so little time for their oversight, who carries herself so wisely and kindly among his people that none are offended—for they have a sense of property in her too which is very pleasant: who advises her husband on every important matter and often restrains him from hasty speech; and who receives him weary, dis-

THE CURE OF SOULS

couraged, irritable, and sends him out again strong, hopeful, sweet-tempered. The woman is in the shadow and the man stands in the open, and it is not till that woman dies and the man is left alone that the people or he himself knows what she has been—for Livingstone is buried in Westminster Abbey, but his wife's grave is in the African forest.

This is the other woman, who is wasteful, extravagant, heedless, who is jealous of her position and full of petty social ambitions, who has an evil or garrulous tongue and creates mischief in all directions, who is ignorant, ill-mannered, offensive, or who is unbelieving and worldly. Such a woman tied to a minister will drive him from church to church, bring reproach upon his name although he be a saint, undo half the good he has wrought, and may drag him down to her own level, till he grow bitter, grasping, suspicious, unmanageable. For in our profession a man

THE MINISTER'S CARE OF HIMSELF

may double or divide his usefulness by his marriage.

The minister's *Household* has a fierce light beating upon it, and must be so governed as to illustrate the Gospel its head preaches. His house must be fair and sweet, like George Herbert's parsonage, but there must not be in it any vain show or soft luxury. He is bound to show hospitality as becomes Christ's minister, but with love and simplicity. His children may not have all the enjoyments of others, although they ought to be heirs of peace, for life in a minister's house hath a certain severity. If the minister be married and have children, as is supposed, then he is not to count himself different from other men and make no *provision* for their maintenance in case of his death. It is his duty to set by a sufficient store for them, that they may not be dependent on charity; and should he be tempted to say that he will leave them penniless to the care of

THE CURE OF SOULS

God, he must not boast of his faith, but understand that he is worse than an infidel. Few things alienate sensible men more quickly from religion than a minister who does not pay his debts or consigns his children to the public. And the minister requires at every turn to deny himself *pleasures* and to mortify innocent fancies lest he should cast a stumbling-block in the way of timid and scrupulous souls—who may be very foolish, but for whom Christ was willing to die. As the minister goeth before on the steep ascent, he must remember the many little children who are following and place his feet in plain safe places.

But chiefly this man must have regard to his soul, that it may be pure and strong, and unto that end he will have to fight, as against all sins; so especially against three which do most easily beset ministers. The first is *laziness*, and as, in a day of high pressure and religious fussing, when

THE MINISTER'S CARE OF HIMSELF

every minister is supposed to be working himself to death, it is easy to make a show of activity, this sin is very insidious and dangerous.

The minister has no hour at which he must begin work, no day through which he is kept at work, no check which shows how much work he has done. His time is at his disposal; his work is his own arranging, he is his own master. If he chooses to idle the day away there is no one to call him to account, except his wife, and she will delight some of his brother ministers by pleading with them to induce her husband not to study so much lest he injure his brain, while they know he does not do two hours' honest study in the week.

[If anything could rouse a sluggard and move him to play the man, it would be his wife's faith in him. All over the world, within and without the ministry, hard-working and self-sacrificing women are covering useless vagabonds and apologising for their faults, and assigning them to ill-health, and prophesying the great things they will yet do. God grant the man may do something for that woman's sake.]

When the minister shuts himself up in his study for a forenoon, nobody except himself and God knows whether he spent the time in work or in lazying about from one book-shelf to another, or in smoking over the newspaper, or in reading the last novel. He goes out to visit at two and comes home at six, and his wife discovers he looks tired, and suggests rest; but he may have spent an hour in one house—to the neglect of four sickrooms, where he was anxiously expected—because the people were agreeable and allowed him to speak about himself.

It is possible to put together a sermon in a few hours—a mere thing of glue and paint—which will please the eye at a distance, and only a few examine any sermon closely.

[Ought a man to preach an old sermon? Yes; if (1) it be a good one; (2) the minister be really unable to produce a new one; (3) if it still fit him so that he can wear it comfortably. For sermons are like clothes, the suit of two years ago is impossible to-day—it ought to be too small.]

Laziness grows on a man, and eats away his morale; he is ashamed in the pulpit, and full of apologies in houses, till at last the people—long-suffering and patient—lose faith in him, and his ministry closes in helplessness and contempt.

The second sin is *unmanliness*, which afflicts many ministers, and for which this excuse can be made, that it is fostered by their circumstances. It is dangerous for any man, however strong and modest he may be, to lay down the law twice every Sunday to audiences who have no right of reply, to be treated with special respect by the majority of people in consequence of his office, to preside frequently over committees whose members are inclined to fall in with his ideas, to be surrounded by women whose piety is apt to make too much of him for his work's sake. Unless he be watchful over himself, and go into the world and meet with men holding other views from his, and have faithful friends to criticise and brace him, he will become intolerant of opposition, autocratic in his tone, furious if resisted, petted if beaten—a peevish child. If a man has been a woman's minister, one dare not differ from him on the weather.

Another corroding and deadening sin is *professionalism*, which shows itself in an affected tone of voice, a studied manner, a use of conventional phrases, and an unholy familiarity with spiritual things. When the minister of Christ falls into this state of soul, it is a woeful tragedy. Conceive

THE MINISTER'S CARE OF HIMSELF

it that a man should receive infants in the name of Christ, should dispense the Sacrament of the Lord's death, should minister by the bedside of the dying, should be witness of the supreme conflicts of the soul, should carry the message of the Divine Love, should intercede for the people with God, should live and work amid sacred mysteries—and should have lost all sense of their awfulness, their loveliness, their tenderness. If any man be able to leave the pulpit without fear, or administer a sacrament without being exhausted, or return from seeing one of his flock pass into eternity, and plunge into society, then he may well ask whether the Spirit of Christ has not forsaken him, and he has not been deposed from his office by the Lord's own hands.

Against those sins and every other the minister's alone protection and defence is the presence of the Lord. In the study of a very fallible and unworthy minister, and above the desk where he writes his sermons, hangs Andrea Del Sarto's head of Christ, the face of One Whose Passion is over, and Who is now alive for evermore, full of peace and majesty. This minister has come to use that picture as a sacrament, in which the mind of the Lord is declared to his heart and conscience with secret approvals and saving judgments. If he consults his own ease and refuses some irksome duty, or through fear of man keeps back the wholesome truth, then is the face of the Master clouded with sadness and disappointment; if, being moved by the Divine Grace, that minister has during the day humbled himself or done some service at a cost to one of the disciples, then is the face lit up with joy, and the eyes of love bid him welcome on his return. The Christ is not in the poor print but in that minister's soul, and it is within we find the Lord before Whom at every moment we stand to be approved or condemned. If

THE MINISTER'S CARE OF HIMSELF

God give us success, then to the feet of Jesus let our sheaves be carried; if it be His will we should fail, to the same dear Lord let us flee, Who knows what it is to see His life fall into the ground and disappear. From His words let us learn to preach; from His example let us learn to serve; in His communion let us find our strength, comfort, peace, Whom not having seen we love, to Whom we shall one day render our account.

www.ingramcontent.com/pod-product-compliance
Lightning Source LLC
Chambersburg PA
CBHW022025240426
43667CB00042B/1192